TEDDY BEAR
Magic

TEDDY BEAR
Magic

Making Adorable Teddy Bears
from Anita Louise's Bearlace Cottage

Anita Louise Crane

A Sterling/Chapelle Book
Sterling Publishing Co., Inc., New York

For *Chapelle Ltd.*
Owner: *Jo Packham*
Staff: *Sandra Anderson, Trice Boerens, Malissa Boatwright, Rebecca Christensen, Holly Fuller, Cherie Hanson, Holly Hollingsworth, Susan Jorgensen, Susan Laws, Amanda B. McPeck, Tammy Perkins, Jamie C. Pierce, Leslie Ridenour, Nancy Whitley, and Lorrie Young*

Photography: *Kevin Dilley/Hazen Photography*
Anita Louise Crane
Photo Styling: *Anita Louise Crane*
Artwork: *Amy Vineyard*

The photographs in this book were taken at the home of the author and at Bearlace Cottage in Park City, Utah.

For information on where to purchase
specialty items in this book, please
write to:

Customer Service Department
Chapelle Ltd.
P.O. Box 9113
Ogden, UT 84409
(801) 621-2777
Fax: (801) 621-2788

Library of Congress Cataloging-in-Publication Data

Crane, Anita Louise.
    Teddy bear magic : making adorable teddy bears from Anita Louise's
Bearlace Cottage / Anita Louise Crane.
        p.   cm.
    "A Sterling/Chapelle book."
    Includes index.
    ISBN 0-8069-0992-7
    1. Soft toy making.   2. Teddy bears.   I. Title.
TT174.3.C73 1995   95-23433
745.592'4—dc20   CIP

10 9 8 7 6 5 4 3 2 1

A Sterling/Chapelle Book

Published by Sterling Publishing Company, Inc.
387 Park Avenue South, New York, N.Y. 10016
© 1995 by Chapelle Ltd.
Distributed in Canada by Sterling Publishing
^c/o Canadian Manda Group, One Atlantic Avenue, Suite 105
Toronto, Ontario, Canada M6K 3E7
Distributed in Great Britain and Europe by Cassell PLC
Villiers House, 41/47 Strand, London WC2N 5JE, England
Distributed in Australia by Capricorn Link (Australia) Pty Ltd.
P.O. Box 6651, Baulkham Hills, Business Center, NSW 2153, Australia
Printed in Hong Kong
All Rights Reserved

Sterling ISBN 0-8069-0992-7

Acknowledgments

I would like to thank my mother, Rose, for the many wonderful stories she told to my brothers and me when we were children. Each story was whimsical and made-up as she went along. They have undoubtedly inspired my creative thinking and a love for imagining Teddy Bears in lifelike situations. My brothers, James and Butchie, I can thank for all the growls from behind doors and for dressing my bears up in cowboy hats and boots. We always had a good laugh. And thanks to my newly found sister, Marie, for her understanding and great sense of humor.

Thank you, Amy Townsend, for your unfailing support in my art and for being my grandma. Thank you, too, for your wonderful family, with such great names to borrow for my bear characters (such as "Henry" and "Emily"), who have made it possible for the Bearlace Cottage to grow.

I appreciate Patsy Blattner for believing in me and helping with all the bear accessories and props, and for waiting so patiently all these years. Thanks to my "bear-body" lady, Marianna, for always responding to "I-need-it-yesterday" projects with great speed and an enjoyable sense of humor. Thanks to my shop angels, Dixie and Charlotte, for helping to keep the shop going while I've been working on this book and for Dixie's lovely bouquets of flowers on my doorstep. Thank you, Carol, for remembering to call me when I needed it most.

To all my children, Ronald, Donald, Robert and Ellen, for being the greatest and giving me 12 wonderful grandchildren, and to Jeremy, for his helpful feedback on the bears. I would like to thank all of my shop's customers and bear's parents for their support and for letting me borrow their "bear children" for photo shoots: Pat Montague, Carol Skeen, Christina of Theodore's Shoppe, Kathy Hughes, and Kathy Pace, for her wonderful antique bears and dolls. Thank you, *Victoria Magazine,* for your wonderful magazine and photography, which has inspired me and contributed immensely to the success of my business.

Thank you, Jo Packham, for making this book possible and Amy Vineyard, for her beautiful renditions of my Teddy Bears. Thank you, Bonnie Barr, for the overtime housecleaning.

I also want to thank my husband, Bruce, whom I love dearly for his patience during the past few years of sharing a house cluttered with stacks of lace, china, and BEARS!

Thanks to "Ophelia" and Michele Durkson Clise for helping me realize that there were indeed other humans out there with a love of Teddy Bears and for all their inspiration. I want them to know that having Aunt Vita at my tea party was the most special day of my life.

And last, but not least, thanks to my cat, Raisen, for his sniff of approval for each bear I create.

I could not have done it without all of you.

Thank you,

Anita

To all my grandchildren:

Holly and Donald
Jennifer, Rachael, Christopher and Jason
Gabrielle and Joshua
Robert and Christopher
Tyson and Kyle

All my Love

About the Author

Inside a cozy Victorian cottage tucked away in the mountains of Park City, Utah, lives a very proper, happy family of bears—and their creator, Anita Louise Crane. At every turn in a forest of antiques and lace, bears with names like Anastasia, Webster and Bodelia can be found having tea, sitting on the love seat, or guarding the house from possible intruders (you never know when Goldilocks may show up again).

Few places could be as packed with as many bears as Anita's house and her store down the road, Bearlace Cottage. If you were to look at all of the bears in both locations, you would soon find that no two bears are exactly alike, even those made from the same patterns. All possess their own character, a trait that has become their creator's trademark. To Anita Louise Crane, each bear is far more than an organized heap of scraps, fur and thread. They are individuals whose personalities take form while being lovingly and individually handcrafted.

The excellence and extra care put into Anita's bears have made them objects of affection for hundreds of proud adoptive "parents," from actor Bruce Willis to husband Bruce Crane, who takes "Grandpa Bear" on all of his business trips.

Anita's career as a designer began during her engagement to Bruce, when, without any formal training, she decided to create her own wedding gown. The wedding photographer blew up the portrait, hung it on the wall of his studio, and soon other brides-to-be were knocking on Anita's door. A special-occasion dress business was born, specializing in lacy fantasy gowns. After a few years of perfecting her sewing skills, Anita accidentally happened upon an antique Teddy Bear. She fell in love with everything but its price, so she decided that with her newly acquired designing and sewing skills, she could make her own. The rest is history.

Her lace and dresses and bears have since been featured in cover stories for *Victoria Magazine*, *Creative Needle*, *Teddy Bear and Friends* and Australia's *Dolls, Bears & Collectibles*. Her bears are also featured in a series of Hallmark cards. Her cherished creations are adopted into happy homes almost as fast as she can make them.

Get out the scissors, needle and thread, and get ready to create some wonderful friends!

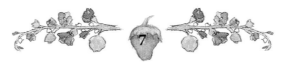

contents

contents

The airing of the TV mini-series "Roots" convinced many Teddy Bears to begin researching their ancestors, or as they prefer to call them, their "fore-bears." Before this time, Teddy Bears had mistakenly taught their cubs that they were descendants of huge grizzly bears who were full of great strength and lived in the tops of the Rocky Mountains, in other famous mountain ranges, and in thick forests. Then the first Teddy Bear historian published his research, and the bear facts came to light: they are really descendants of small woolen bears who were full of straw and lived on the tops of children's beds, in their toy chests, and in their hearts.

Fortunately, it appears that none of today's Teddy Bears were bothered by this revelation. Most of them thought it was too cold in the mountains anyway, plus they were certain that they could get more hugs sitting at home than they ever could elsewhere.

Nevertheless, the research of that historian, Mr. Carl Sanbear, did show that the origin of the name "Teddy Bear" was indeed due to a real bear. It was not a brave bear from the Rocky Mountains, however; this famous cub's only feat was to look harmless and frightened as it sat tied to a Mississippi tree in 1902. Not far from this frightened bear stood the President of the United States, "Teddy" Roosevelt, who was nearing the end of an unsuccessful bear-hunting expedition. Despite the encouragement of hunting partners who had cornered the bear for him, Roosevelt refused to shoot the helpless cub.

As time went on and Teddy Bears continued to grow in popularity, their shape also evolved. At first, the older generation of Teddy Bears learned to be tolerant of the refinements in the new generation of bears. Earlier bears had pointed muzzles, humped backs, and long limbs. Gradually, bear faces widened up, humps began to disappear, and limbs grew short and stubby.

This incident was later illustrated in the *Washington Post* by political cartoonist Clifford K. Berryman. Subsequent cartoons featured the little bear as a symbol of the President, and within a year the cartoon bear had been transformed into a children's toy–the Teddy Bear.

The years 1903 to 1908 were what Mr. Sanbear called the "Bear-Boomer" years, when numerous toy companies turned their attention to making Teddy Bears. During this period, "adoption" rates went from 12,000 to 975,000 Teddy Bears a year. At the same time, Teddy Bears were being featured in books, newspaper articles, mugs, and spoons.

But not all changes were refinements. The main topic of discussion at Teddy Bear tea parties was the startling evolution from natural-colored mohair to synthetic furs and less realistic colors. Many Teddy Bear leaders were concerned that before long, the rising generation would grow up to be nothing but a bunch of fat, artificial, unjointed, mass-produced whippersnappers!

The moral decline of the new generation

culminated in 1964, when the first fully machine-washable bear was introduced. (This was also the year "Beatlemania" arrived in the United States. Many bears claim this was no coincidence.) But the rebellious Teddy Bears of the "Synthetic Revolution" had grown up by the 1980s, and political circles turned again to discussion of "Traditional Teddy Values."

To some, this phrase referred to the value of quality antique bears. For example, in 1989, a Steiff Teddy Bear was auctioned at Sotheby's for $86,000. Numerous Teddy Bear museums and conventions began to dot the globe, along with several collector's magazines.

But to most adoptive parents of Teddy Bears, the talk of values meant the importance of spending not money but "quality time" with their bears, not

only in their finished state, but in their formative stages as well. Because of this, a cottage industry, dedicated to the making of unique, collectible, jointed bears from traditional materials, is beginning to thrive. Thousands of people are learning to make bears in their own homes. The traditional bear, with some modern refinements, has made its return!

Introduction

One rainy afternoon, while I was shopping for linens and lace, I ducked under an awning to get out of the rain. The pink-and-white striped awning hung out over a charming little shop whose window was occupied by antique bears and dolls having tea at a child-size wicker table and chairs. One of the little bears caught my eye and stole my heart. I can still see those black eyes looking up at me. He was lovingly worn and had little sprigs of excelsior sticking out of holes in his feet. His head drooped a bit and was turned at an angle, which made him appear to be saying, "Won't you please take me home?"

I entered the shop and inquired as to the procedure for and price of adopting one of the bears in the window. I was soon to find out his adoption fee was much more than I could afford. I left that shop, but to this day, when I close my eyes, I can still see "my little Teddy Bear".

Several months later on a rainy afternoon, again while shopping, I saw a newly sewn bear in a department store window. I realized at that moment that I truly had missed the "forest for the trees"! I could make a new "antique" Teddy Bear of my own. I returned home immediately and began. I designed my own pattern, but when I finished my first little friend was a fright! It looked more like a monkey than an antique bear. After much searching, I found a preprinted pattern that I could use, added my own personal touches, and the result was a bear that was indeed similar to the one in the antique wicker chair in the window. The next step was to try again to create my own original patterns–and with success I became hooked! Now with each bear I make, I see the "magic" take over as a new Teddy Bear is born.

I hope you will find the photographs and patterns in this book inspiring and enjoyable. Whether you actually sew a bear or purchase one and dress it in antique clothing, I think you will find much happiness in this romantic and whimsical world.

Anita Louise Crane

Materials

Furs

Of all the furs below, I find "distressed" or "vintage" mohair to be the most satisfactory for my designs. Mohair, made from the wool of the Angora goat, is the traditional fur used for antique bears. It is available in many different lengths, colors and nap styles, and is even available mixed with silk. Although it is much more expensive than synthetic furs, the feel and workability far exceed those of synthetic.

Wool•Mohair•Alpaca•String Mohair•
Synthetic, Viscose and cotton piles

You should make your first bear from a less expensive fur, and then move up to a more expensive fabric. Wool and Alpaca are also expensive.

You can dye your own white fur and tint it yourself with dye or tea. You can also use natural dyes such as walnuts, berries, or berry soft drinks. Always practice on small pieces first.

Stuffing

Polyester Stuffing
Polyester or dacron stuffing are the most commonly used in bear-making today, and the most readily available. I find that lower quality stuffing works well for hard-stuffed bears. Try different brands and use the one you like. Some are more springy, and others are better suited to soft bears.

Excelsior (Straw)
Used in very early antique bears. One of the bear designs in this book is stuffed with excelsior, and its head is a mixture of polyester filling and excelsior. This stuffing is difficult to work with and is messy. It does give a wonderful "old" feel to new bears. I do not recommend it for those with allergies or for children's toys.

When stuffing with excelsior, cut the pieces smaller with scissors and do the stuffing outside the house. It is very messy to work with, and birds will appreciate having access to the small pieces of straw.

Plastic Beads
Very small plastic beads can be used to make a saggy, floppy bear. It will make the bear very heavy. I have used it just in the bottom of the body for weight and for helping the bear to sit better. It is not recommended for children's toys. Heads are always stuffed with polyester stuffing.

Scraps of Fur
I like to use fur scraps in the body of the bear for weight and for spare fur in the event it loses an ear or needs a repair. I mix it with polyester stuffing or excelsior for a smooth finish.

Eyes

Antique bears usually only have shoe-button eyes. Glass eyes were used after 1910. These glass eyes are available today in black, brown, blue, green, etc. A small quantity of original shoe-button eyes are also available.

For a traditional "old style," it is good to use the glass eyes. However, glass eyes can break, or can be pulled out by an inquisitive child and cause harm. If you are making a Teddy Bear for a child, it is much safer to use safety-lock plastic eyes. One drawback is that they must be installed before stuffing the head.

If Teddy's eyes look too shiny and new and you want them to look like well-worn shoe buttons, just put some hand cream on your hands and rub his eyes. The shine will tone down a bit.

Paw Pads

I like to use traditional heavy wool felt. This felt is available in many colors to match your fur. However, you may like to use suede or ultra-suede for a richer appearance. Some designers also use leather. Squares of felt are available at most fabric and craft stores; you will find the quality of wool to be superior to other types of synthetic felt.

Growlers

Growlers and squeakers are used so that your bear can "talk." They are available through bear supply companies and many craft stores. Always put the growler in a little cotton sack so that the stuffing does not ruin the noise mechanism.

Joints

Each joint requires two disks and two washers plus jointing hardware. Instructions for each individual bear list the diameter of disks needed; the diameter of the disk holes will be decided by the width of the jointing hardware you choose.

Disks

If you plan to make a lot of bears, look into either the lock-nut or cotter pin systems for long-term durability and traditional use.

These are made of either pressed wood or cardboard and are available through bear supply companies and some hardware stores. When purchasing, specify both the diameter of the disks and the diameter of their holes (¼" or ⅛" to accommodate the hardware you choose). Disks can also be made with heavy cardboard or plastic. For long-term durability, I suggest using only wood, Masonite or cardboard.

Lock-nuts

This is the method I prefer. It consists of a lock-nut, a bolt and two washers. This system

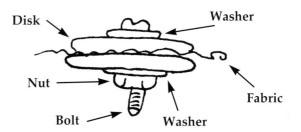

Lock-nut

Cotter pin

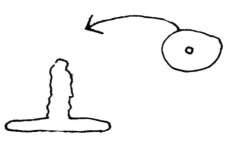

Snap-on joint

requires two wrenches for tightening. When I purchased my first joint set, I took it to the hardware store to find the correct sizes of wrenches.

Cotter Pins

A metal pin available at most hardware stores and Teddy Bear supply companies. Requires needle-nose pliers.

Plastic Doll Snap-on Joints

I used these for several years because they are simple to use and are readily available at most craft stores.

Pop Rivets

Used mostly by large Teddy Bear manufacturers because the required tools are complicated and expensive.

Tools

Awl
Use this, a seam ripper, or a large needle for punching holes for joints and eyes.

Basting Needle
Always baste before machine stitching. It will save you hours of pulling stitches.

Carpet/Buttonhole Thread
Its strength is good for hand-sewing openings closed and sewing in the eyes. Dental floss also works quite well.

Embroidery Needle
Needed for creating nose and mouth.

Fur-Grooming Brush
Is needed for brushing fur out of seams during the sewing process. A wire dog or cat brush works well.

Hot Glue Gun
I use it for securing the bolt in the head. Many bear makers prefer leaving an opening in the bottom of the head and using two wrenches; if you do this, you will not need hot glue.

Long Needle
A 7" to 12" needle will save you a lot of trouble when you are trying to sew eyes into an already-stuffed head.

Mustache-Trimming Scissors
Used for trimming fur around snout and eyes.

Needle-Nose Pliers:
Good for bending wires on certain eye styles and when using cotter pins or joints. Also good for pulling out embroidery floss.

Scissors
Used for cutting fur and felt. Make sure the tips are sharp, because they are the only part you should use with the fur. Cut only the backing, not the fur.

Sewing Machine with Heavy-Duty Needle
Even if you do brush your fur well, a heavy needle will be needed.

Stick Pins
For positioning ears.

Stuffing Stick
Professional sticks are available, but wooden spoon handles and chopsticks are an adequate substitute.

Tracing Paper
For transferring patterns from book.

Wire Cutter
Useful for cutting excess wire from some types of eyes.

Wrenches
For lock-nut jointing, you will need wrenches or nut-drivers. Other methods require none.

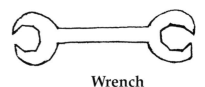

Wrench

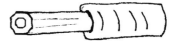

Nut-driver

General Instructions

The Pattern

1. Trace pattern pieces onto strong cardboard or poster board. One method is to trace the pattern onto tracing paper, and then cut out the pattern and use to trace onto the cardboard. Cut out the cardboard pattern pieces.

2. Transfer all markings, such as opening placements, darts, joint locations and nap direction (direction the fur lays).

When laying out the pattern on the fur, follow the direction of the nap as illustrated on the pattern. When laying out the head, you can turn the fur over and then try to place the gusset piece so that a curl or wrinkle is right between the eyes. Do the same with side head pieces. A little curl around the eye area can do a great deal for Teddy's expression. I have also occasionally cut the center gusset with the nap going down instead of back. This creates a more scruffy looking (boy) bear.

When I am finished with my patterns, I string them on a ribbon and hang them on a hook.

Step 2

Cutting the Fur

1. Lay out pattern pieces on back of the fur fabric, checking carefully for nap directions. It helps to mark an arrow on the back of the fur in the direction of the nap with a pencil. To determine the nap direction, you simply smooth your hand across the fur to see which way the fur lays.

2. Pin the pattern pieces to the fabric or hold them in place as you trace around them with a pencil or water-soluble pen. Be careful to reverse left and right pattern pieces.

3. Now you are ready to cut the pieces. Using the tips of the scissors, make little snips, cutting the backing of the fur only.

4. Match up the left and right pieces. Check to see that you have all the sections. Now you are ready to create your bear.

Step 3

Sewing the Head

All pattern pieces have a built-in ⅛" seam allowance. Many sewing machines show a measurement on the foot of the machine to allow accurate stitching. If yours does not, mark the seam allowance on the machine with a piece of tape.

Always baste before machine sewing. This can save you many hours of frustrating seam removal. As you sew, so you rip!

1. Sew darts together, if applicable, to make the head rounded.

2. Pin two head pieces right sides together. Sew from top of snout to bottom of front neck, or A to B.

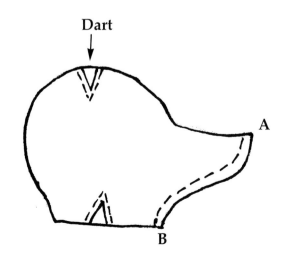

Dart

A

B

3. Baste the gusset piece to the top of both sides of the head (A to C). Machine-stitch to make more secure.

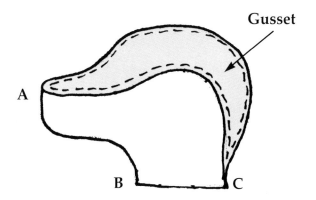

Gusset

A

B   C

4. Machine-stitch rest of head, except for opening from B to C. Always check front and back of stitching to make sure you have caught both sides of the fabric. Turn and brush seams.

Use a pet wire brush for brushing the fur in place as you sew (special wire brushes are also available from most Teddy Bear suppliers). It is very helpful in keeping fur away from the seams. Stubborn fur can be pulled out with a large needle. I find brushing Teddy's face makes a rather angry looking bear softer and more pleasant.

5. Now you can sew the ears together. Cut out ears from fabric, two left, two right (the ear patterns are not all symmetrical, even though they look like it). Pin opposite pieces right sides together and sew from A to B, around the curve and then turn ear right side out.

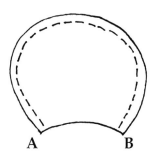

A   B

6. Brush out the seams and then trim the center front of each ear. Close bottom of ear with ladder stitch. The ear is sewn onto the head after the head is stuffed.

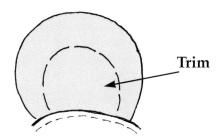

Trim

When knotting off thread after sewing openings shut, try wrapping the thread around the needle three times, slipping it down to form a knot, and pulling it through the fur. Repeat this once more so that your knot will not pull through.

Step 4
Stuffing the Head

1. Starting at the tip of the snout, stuff the head. Holding the snout on the outside with one hand, stuff the snout with small pieces of polyester stuffing, forming as you go with your outside hand. Be sure there are not any air spaces in the stuffing.

2. Continue stuffing between the eyes and the forehead; then stuff the cheeks and the back of the head.

3. Go back and firm up the snout by inserting small pieces with a stuffing stick. Continue until the snout is quite firm (a poorly stuffed snout will make embroidering the nose very difficult). When you are satisfied with the shape and stuffing, you are ready to create the face. I like to finish the head before sewing the rest of the bear so that it can be placed in a teacup and accompany me while I assemble the body. Of course, this step is entirely up to you.

These photos demonstrate how different eye sizes and ear placement affect your bear's appearance. Left: Small eyes, ears up high. Right: Large eyes, ears further back.

Step 5
Creating the Face

Mark the eye placement by using straight pins with beaded heads. You can move the pins around until you are satisfied with the placement, or put them exactly where the pattern is marked.

Close together: Younger looking
Far apart: Older and wiser
Large Eyes: Younger looking
Small eyes: Older and wiser

Sewing in the Eyes

Safety plastic eyes are attached before stuffing (See manufacturers instructions). Glass eyes are sewn in after the head is completely stuffed.

1. Thread the metal loop of the eye with strong, doubled thread. Tie a knot in the thread, just below the loop. Squeeze the loop together with pliers for easy insertion. You should have a tail of thread about 1 foot long.

2. Thread a 7" to 12" needle with all 4 threads of the tail. Insert needle into the space marked for the eye, coming out at the ear area on the opposite side of the head.

3. With only two threads on the needle, make a small stitch next to where the thread is coming out. Knot all 4 threads together, pulling them tightly so the eye is pulled in and forms an eye socket. The indentation made in the ear area will eventually be covered by the ear.

4. Rethread the needle with the tails of all 4 threads and stitch through the stuffing, moving from the ear indentation down to the neck area. Knot off tightly. Repeat for other eye.

Trimming the Nose

1. Using small scissors (mustache-trimming scissors from any drugstore work well), make small snips from the nose to the eye area. Take great care, as the fur will not grow back!

2. Following the photo of the bear, trim fur on sides of the snout and under the chin. Snip the fur in the direction it lays so that you have no sharp edges. This takes practice. Try not to cut the fur too short at first. You can always go back and trim it shorter after you are finished.

Embroidering the Nose

I have not provided full-size templates because there are too many variables when working with a bear. Depending on how you have stuffed or sewn your bear, plus your embroidery style, a pre-made nose template could cause you more frustration than making your own template based on one of the below styles. Besides, if your goal is to make a one-of-a-kind Teddy, you want to use the style most suited to your bear's future personality.

1. Thread a large embroidery needle with the desired color of cotton floss. For best results, use a single thread.

2. Cut a piece of felt from leftover scraps of felt, in the desired nose shape. Make sure you have already cut your paw pad. You will want to experiment with the scraps until you find the shape and size you want. This will be your template to help you to stay in the lines, and will make a nice pad for the stitching. I like to try several different styles until I find the one best suited for the Teddy I am working on.

3. Baste or glue the template in position where it gives the most expression. Below are examples of the most common types of nose and mouth patterns. Any of them can be used for any of the bears.

4. Carefully embroider the nose and mouth, following the pattern. Keep your tension even and tight and untwist threads as you go. If the fur around the nose pulls into the stitches, try holding down the muzzle fur with removable sticky tape, or trim it a little more.

If you are ever not satisfied with the appearance, snip the embroidered pieces and pull them out with needle-nose pliers. If there is ever any part of the bear I find myself redoing, it is nose embroidery, so don't worry if the look isn't quite right the first time. Keep cutting and restitching until you like it.

I always try several different mouth styles when I embroider the nose. You can even embroider a smile on the bear.

5. Do not knot the thread when you are finished. Catch the thread in a backstitch, hiding it in the nose threads.

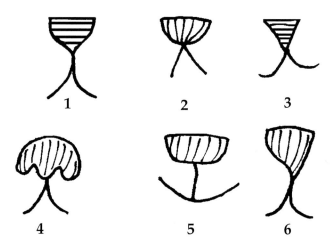

Nose and mouth styles

Sewing the Ears

1. Move the ears around, pinning them in place to see how your bear's personality changes with the placement. Use pins to hold the ears in place while you look at your bear close up and at a distance.

2. Using heavy carpet or buttonhole thread, sew the bottom of the ears (A to B in diagram on bottom of page 20) in place using a ladder stitch. Curve the ears as you stitch. Knot the thread and pull knot into head. Cut off excess thread. Repeat for other ear.

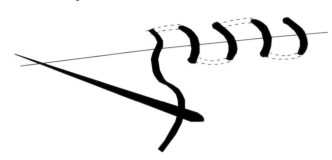

Ladder stitch

I have noticed that ears which are not perfectly placed give the bear more expression. One ear up or held forward looks so cute. I like to place ears slightly low and to the back of the head.

Step 6
Sewing the Body, Arms and Legs

Always pin and baste first; then machine-stitch. Sew double seams or use forward-backward stitch on the machine. Always check for missed edges. As you baste or sew, push fur aside so as not to sew over the fur on the outside. Brush with wire brush after turning, and pull fur from seams with needle. Do this right away, as fur will become crushed permanently if you leave it in the seam too long.

Body

1. Where applicable, pin left and right back pieces together. Sew from top to bottom, leaving opening where marked.

2. Pin left and right front pieces together. Sew from top to bottom of front.

3. With right sides facing, pin front section to back section, matching side seams. Starting at top, sew all the way around.

4. Turn right side out. Brush seams and pull stubborn fur out of seams with large needle.

Arms

1. Pin inside arm to paw pad; machine-stitch.

2. With right sides facing, pin outside arm to inside arm and stitch together all the way around, leaving opening where marked in pattern piece.

3. Turn arm right side out and brush seams. Pull fur out of seams with needle where necessary.

4. Repeat for other arm.

Legs

1. With right sides facing, pin right and left side legs together. Stitch pieces together, leaving opening where marked.

2. Pin foot pad to leg and baste all the way around the pad, easing the curves as you stitch. Machine-sew.

3. Turn right side out, brush and pull fur out of seams with needle where necessary.

4. Repeat for other leg.

Step 7
Assembling the Bear Joints

I like to stuff the paws and feet before jointing. However, this step can be completed after the bear is completely jointed.

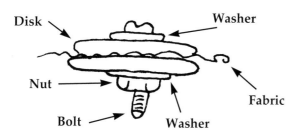

Disk **Washer**

Nut

Fabric

Bolt **Washer**

Proper lock-nut assembly

Always joint the head to the body first. Each joint consists of two disks and washers and one of the following jointing mechanisms: nuts and bolts, cotter pins, pop-rivets or plastic snap-on joints. All can be purchased from Teddy Bear supply companies. Most hardware stores carry cotter pins with compatible washers. When ordering, make sure all pieces match.

Jointing Head to Body
The following instructions demonstrate the use of lock-nuts and bolts. The procedure is essentially the same for the other jointing mechanisms.

Position of head joint

1. Using carpet or buttonhole thread, gather the neck and pull tightly around the neck joint. The neck joint will consist of one bolt and a washer and disk. The washer is placed on the screw before the disk.

I put a little hot glue at the base of the bolt so that when I tighten the joint, the screw does not slip. Tighten the thread around the washer and knot several times. Trim any bulky areas that might interfere with the process.

2. Punch hole in the body with an awl where the head is to be placed. Insert the head bolt (the part sticking out of the head) into the body. Insert another disk and washer inside the body over the bolt and screw on nut. Tighten the nut with a wrench or nut-driver (see diagram, page 18). The glue applied to the bolt top should keep the other end of the bolt from slipping.

If the glue does not hold, simply open the seam at the back of the head and insert a wrench to hold the end of the bolt while you tighten the nut inside the body. When finished, close seam with ladder stitch. You may omit the glue step if you wish. You could also use a cotter pin instead of a bolt for head jointing.

For easy positioning of the bear's head for expression, I prefer that the neck joints be a bit looser than other joints. Sometimes I use a small disk inside the body when attaching the head so that the head tilts a little.

Arms and Legs
1. Hold the legs onto the body and check if the joint markings from the pattern are precisely where you want them. Do the same for the arms so that they are not placed too high or too far back or forward. Generally, the best position is just in back of the side seam.

2. Insert a screw, disk and washer into the inside of each leg. Insert leg into the marked placement for leg on the body, and repeat as

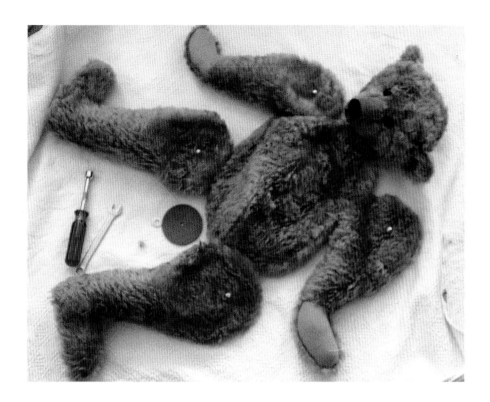

All limbs jointed, ready for assembly

above. Glue is not needed on the limb joints, as you can hold both sides of the joint with wrenches or nut drivers.

If the joints are too loose, you will have to remove the stuffing from the body and the limbs and redo. To avoid this, tighten the joints as tightly as you can and then back off one turn. The joint will seem too tight; however, when you finish stuffing, they will loosen up because the stuffing puts tension on the fur.

Stuffing the body

1. When using polyester stuffing, always use little pieces of stuffing, and methodically stuff from the tip of the paw to the opening. If the pieces are too large, the bear will appear lumpy. When the stuffing moves (and it will), a larger piece will move in a larger space. It is logical that small pieces moving individually will leave smaller air spaces.

Stuff fur scraps in the belly or hump of your bear so that you will have fur for any emer-

gency repairs. If you give Teddy for a gift, pass this information on to its new parent. To help your bear sit better, put about ½ to 1 cup of plastic pellets (within a muslin sack) in the bottom of the body, then continue stuffing with the polyester stuffing. DO NOT use plastic pellets for children's toys.

It is extremely difficult to go back and try to fill in the tip of a paw or foot. You will probably have to pull all the stuffing out and start over. If you like a soft bear, stuff the paws and feet hard and lighten up as you move up the limb. Always stuff the head firmly.

2. Finish stuffing the bear, molding and rounding out the limbs and body as you stuff. After you are satisfied, close the openings with a ladder stitch (See page 23), burying the knot in the fur.

Miss Marigold

The lovely Miss Marigold is an accomplished seamstress who sits for long hours at her sewing machine.

In a room that is so crowded she is sometimes lost for days, she designs and creates only heirloom quality objects d'art. Her creations begin with the most elegant of wedding dresses for young bride-bears-to-be and from the leftover scraps (Miss Marigold never wastes anything), she fashions accents for every room in the house.

Because she spends so much time at the sewing machine, she often complains about headaches. When this happens, she must stop everything she is doing and go off to her scented feather bed, which is covered with her much-loved antique linens and lace. Miss Marigold always says that a

cup of herbal tea (with lots of extra honey), a little lavender and rosemary slipped underneath her pillow (to scent her sleep and her dreams), and a little rest will make her headache go away.

Some of the other bears say she gets an awful lot of headaches, and have suggested that a faster-acting remedy would allow her to go back to work more quickly. Those who know Miss Marigold best, and have tasted her tea and smelled the scent of spring that fills her room, say it is a wonder that Miss Marigold does not get headaches more often!

Miss Marigold Materials
(14" Bear)

Fur
⅜ yd. brown short vintage finish mohair

Stuffing
12 oz. bag polyester stuffing

Eyes
8 mm black glass eyes

Paws
Two squares or ⅛ yd. tan wool felt

Joints
10 disks, 1½"-diameter
Materials for five sets of joints (See *General Instructions* for options)

Other Materials
Black embroidery floss for nose
Heavy carpet or buttonhole thread, for closing openings and sewing in eyes
Sewing thread to match fur

Tools
Awl or large needle for punching holes for joints and eyes
Basting needle
Embroidery needle
Fur-grooming brush (dog or cat brush works well)
Hot glue gun for neck joint (optional)
Mustache trimmers for trimming fur
Needle-nose pliers (optional)
Scissors
Sewing machine with heavy-duty needle
Stick pins for positioning ears
Stuffing stick or wooden spoon
Tools as required for chosen jointing system
Tracing paper and pencil for transferring pattern from book
7" to 12" needle for sewing in eyes

Finishing

Begin by reading the *General Instructions* on pages 19–25. Cut fur according to patterns on pages 30–33. Follow the *General Instructions* for sewing and assembly. Trim nose according to photograph. Sew four claws on paws and feet with black floss.

Miss Marigold's sister-in-law, Miss Potter (photo on page 46), is made from the same pattern, using the same techniques. The only difference is she is made out of an inexpensive plush fur and materials most of us have in our sewing closets! I added an old lace scrap for her shawl and held it together with a pretty button I found at a local fabric shop.

I antiqued Marigold's fur and paws by giving her a sponge bath with tea (a cup of any flavored tea, chilled, will work). I trimmed the fur on her paws and feet short to better show the individual "fingers," and to make her look older than she really is. None of the other bears know Miss Marigold's true age, but that doesn't keep them from guessing. Marigold tells them she's young and energetic enough to climb to the top of the the tallest spruce, and old and wise enough to keep all four feet on the ground!

Miss Marigold has several antique outfits that are actually antique doll clothing. The shawls are made from lace collars; the pretty little antique hats can be made easily with a crafts-store straw hat and silk flowers applied with a glue gun.

Teddy Bear Tips

Old children's' china, furniture and toys are wonderful display items for your Teddy. I have used these types of props throughout the book. It doesn't take long to get an eye for bear display items.

Many manufacturers are now producing wonderful tiny teapots and teacups. Some even look like they have tea in them. Check local gift shops and crafts stores.

None of Miss Marigold's friends wonder why she gets so many headaches. In fact, as of late, her friends have frequently complained about headaches themselves, while visiting at her house for afternoon tea. Miss Marigold always takes care of them with a wink and a smile.

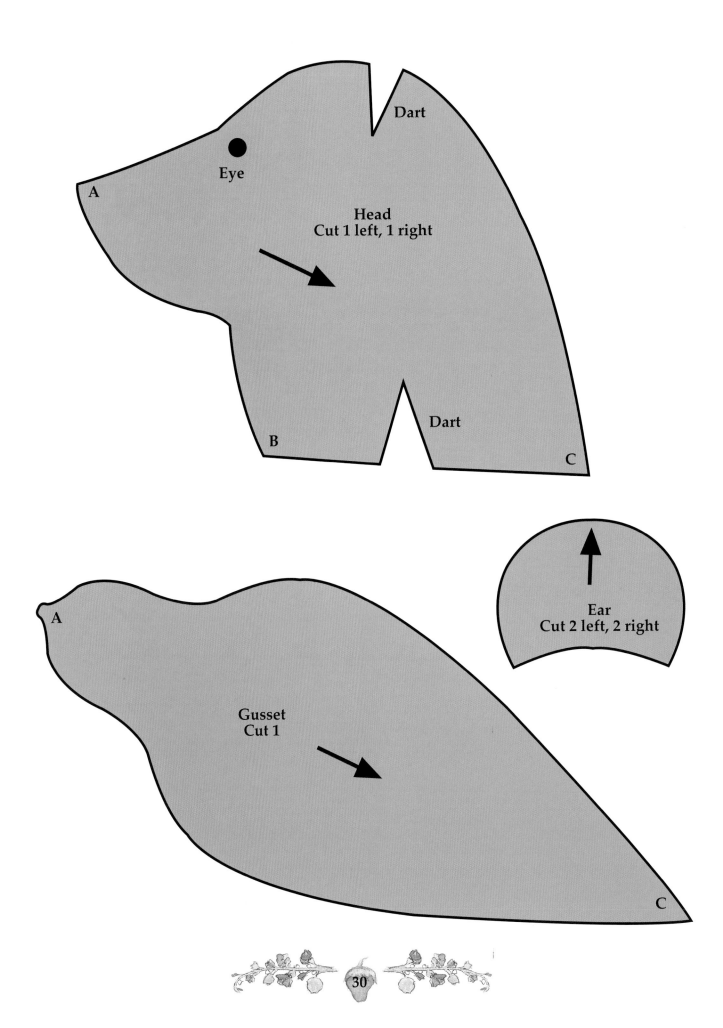

Dart

Eye

A

Head
Cut 1 left, 1 right

Dart

B

C

A

Gusset
Cut 1

C

Ear
Cut 2 left, 2 right

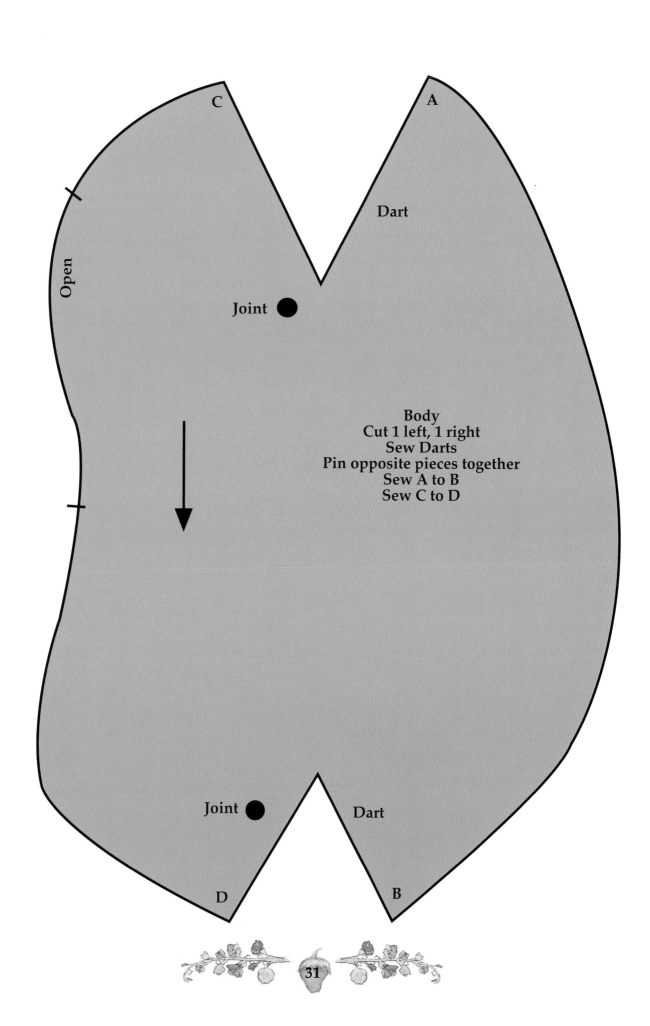

C

A

Dart

Open

Joint ●

Body
Cut 1 left, 1 right
Sew Darts
Pin opposite pieces together
Sew A to B
Sew C to D

Joint ●

Dart

D

B

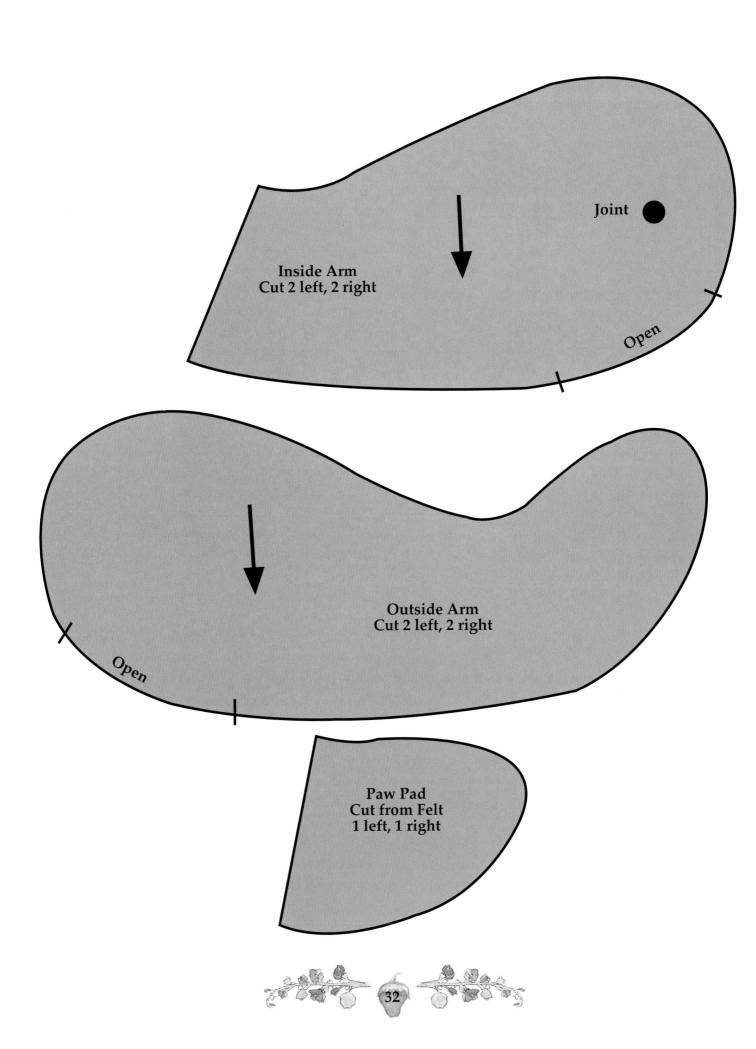

Inside Arm
Cut 2 left, 2 right

Joint

Open

Outside Arm
Cut 2 left, 2 right

Open

Paw Pad
Cut from Felt
1 left, 1 right

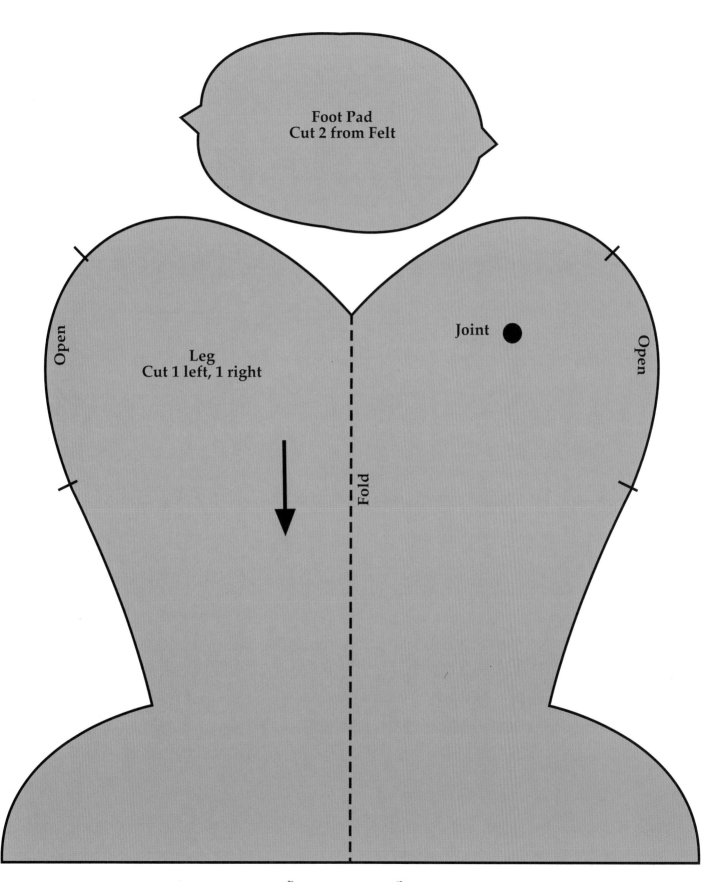

Foot Pad
Cut 2 from Felt

Open

Leg
Cut 1 left, 1 right

Joint

Open

Fold

Miss Pansy

Miss Pansy loves tea even more than other bears, so much that she has tea several times a day.

Her tea is usually served on a silver tray with nice lace napkins, with large helpings of scones and shortbread, and with Miss Pansy's favorite French vanilla ice cream topped with lots of honey. Her love for tea time and all its trimmings has helped Miss Pansy acquire a rather large waistline, but she doesn't care. It's okay to be chubby when you are a Teddy Bear, she says, because it makes you more cuddly. She points out that even though she is no bear size 5, she is in very good shape because she walks and runs every day, and her posture is also quite good.

On special occasions, Miss Pansy can be seen wearing her Aunt Ellyn's antique brooch that has been in her family for many generations. Aunt Ellyn gave it to Miss Pansy on her bear-school graduation day (Pansy got straight A's in home economics). Miss Pansy also loves to wear pretty lace dresses and pink shoes. (She did have to take the buttons off the shoes so that they wouldn't be too tight for her large feet.) Miss Pansy is, also, most fond of fancy hats, but oftentimes she simply cannot make up her mind as to which one she should wear.

TIP LEWIS
AND HIS LAMP

Miss Pansy Materials
(14" Bear)

Fur
⅜ yd. pink short-pile mohair

Stuffing
12 oz. bag polyester stuffing

Eyes
8 mm black glass eyes on loop

Paws
Two squares or ⅛ yd. tan wool felt

Joints
10 disks, 1½"-diameter
Materials for five sets of joints (See *General Instructions* for options)

Other Materials
Black embroidery floss for nose
Heavy carpet or buttonhole thread, for closing openings and sewing in eyes
Sewing thread to match fur

Tools
Awl or large needle for punching holes for joints and eyes
Basting needle
Embroidery needle
Fur-grooming brush (dog or cat brush works well)
Hot glue gun for neck joint (optional)
Mustache trimmers for trimming fur
Needle-nose pliers (optional)
Scissors
Sewing machine with heavy-duty needle
Stick pins for positioning ears
Stuffing stick or wooden spoon
Tools as required for chosen jointing system
Tracing paper and pencil for transferring pattern from book
7" to 12" needle for sewing in eyes.

Finishing

Begin by reading the *General Instructions* on pages 19–25. Cut fur according to patterns on pages 30–33. Follow the *General Instructions* for sewing and assembly. Trim nose according to photograph.

To make a skirt for Pansy, gather an 18" x 7" piece of fabric to the measurement of her waist. Add a waistband of fabric or ribbon. Add an antique or new lace collar and a shawl and button as a brooch.

Little straw hats and shoes are available at most crafts stores. You can add pretty ribbons and flowers with a glue gun. You might want to embroider the nose with pink floss instead and make the paw pads to match in pink or purple felt.

Pansy has a cousin named Mushroom that looks a lot like her, except that he is a boy, and he has no fur whatsoever (photo on page 47). He is made using the same pattern and techniques as Pansy, except that he is made entirely of paw-pad materials! He also has an eyebrow stitch at the sides of his eyes, and embroidered claws on his paws and feet. Mushroom prefers to wear nothing more than a bow tie when he goes to market for flowers.

Teddy Bear Tips

Keep lace collar attached to your bear by sewing on a button. Many beautiful buttons are available at sewing stores and some antique stores.

Having a hard time thinking of an appropriate name for your Teddy? Old flower books have wonderful girl names. Ask about your ancestors. Go through the kitchen cupboard and think "How about Brie? ... Oatmeal? ... Lemon?"

Miss Pansy still refuses to follow a diet, but most of the other Teddy Bears agree she would not be nearly as popular or as cuddly if she did!

Norman

Norman spends as much time as possible in his authentic French country kitchen baking pies stuffed full of berries and topped with the fanciest of pie crusts.

His very favorite, of course, is the blueberry cobbler made from his grandmother's recipe.

In the beginning, when Norman first learned the art of baking, he would wear his mother's apron to keep flour off his belly. Now, however, that he is a graduate of the culinary institute and has become a master baker in his own right, his mother has made him his own blueberry-colored apron. Norman likes this particular color blue so much that he doesn't even mind when the blueberries stain his fur.

Right outside Norman's kitchen window a small bird, named Blueberry, has a nest. At first, Norman liked Blueberry because of his color, but lately he is not so sure. For one thing, Blueberry only seems to appear and begin his morning songs when the scent of fresh-baked pies fills the air. Norman is generous with his pies, but likes to invite friends over only after they have cooled.

Norman is especially annoyed when Blueberry lands on his head while he is very carefully taking the pies from the oven. He usually responds with a menacing growl, but Blueberry never stops singing, and has not yet returned to his nest without a fresh, hot piece of pie crust with blueberries stuck to the top.

Norman Materials
(14" Bear)

Fur
⅜ yd. short-pile synthetic fur

Stuffing
12 oz. bag polyester stuffing

Eyes
8 mm black eyes

Paws
Two squares or ⅛ yd. tan wool felt

Joints
10 disks, 1½"-diameter
Materials for five sets of joints (See *General Instructions* for options)

Other Materials
Black embroidery floss for nose
Heavy carpet or buttonhole thread, for closing openings and sewing in eyes
Sewing thread to match fur

Tools
Awl or large needle for punching holes for joints and eyes
Basting needle
Embroidery needle
Fur-grooming brush (dog or cat brush works well)
Hot glue gun for neck joint (optional)
Mustache trimmers for trimming fur
Needle-nose pliers (optional)
Scissors
Sewing machine with heavy-duty needle
Stick pins for positioning ears
Stuffing stick or wooden spoon
Tools as required for chosen jointing system
Tracing paper and pencil for transferring pattern from book
7" to 12" needle for sewing in eyes.

Finishing

Wash the synthetic fur pile and hang it on the line to dry so that the wrinkles will stay in the fabric. This gives the fur an antique/distressed appearance. Read the *General Instructions* on pages 19–25. Cut fur according to pattern on pages 30–33. Follow the *General Instructions* for sewing and assembly. Trim nose according to photograph.

When Norman was finished, he had a cool tea bath with a sponge (the "bath" is made from a cup of tea of any flavor, cooled down). Norman loves his bath and usually laughs and giggles the entire time. The bath gives his coat the look of experience and age, further adding to his antique appearance. I suggest that you experiment with a scrap of fur first for the amount of antiquing you desire. After his bath, let him dry on the porch or kitchen drain board. Norman prefers having something to read while he dries. He likes *Gourmet* magazine a lot, although he only looks at the pictures.

Cut little holes in his paws and stitch them or brush them for a worn appearance. You might also sew on little patches with print materials or matching felt. Add a bow tie of ribbon or fabric and Norman is ready for the day. Norman should always appear worn and well loved (probably from being kissed a lot).

Teddy Bear Tips

Old baby shoes are great on Teddy Bears. I find that putting the shoe on the leg before stuffing it makes it much easier to obtain a good fit.

Help Teddy reach the table by sitting it on a book, pillow or hat boxes. You can also hide a hat box under a long skirt so that your bear looks taller. Most bear-supply companies and crafts stores have bear and doll stands to hold your bear upright.

Norman still enjoys baking pies, but has closed the window to his kitchen so that Blueberry must stay outside and sing his songs. But even though Blueberry and his antics drive Norman crazy, he still loves Blueberry enough to bring a hot, tiny piece of pie to his nest every afternoon.

Gooseberry

You see, Gooseberry, or Goose to his friends, is a little red bear who, in his youth, travelled all over the world. Unfortunately, he never got to see much of it.

As a baby, he was adopted by a rich little girl named Nettie, who was very spoiled. She had so many toys that poor Goose spent most trips hidden away in a cardboard trunk made especially for him.

Today, Nettie is grown with children of her own, and even though Goose is really quite old himself, he looks much younger than his years–due to the fact that he never got out much. He may be a mature bear, but because he grew up alone, spending countless afternoons with only the characters from the pages in the books that he so loved to read, he is so shy that he hides when Nettie's noisy children are about. One day, he hid in the flour bin and managed to nap there for a whole week!

One sunny afternoon not so long ago, while hiding from the children and skipping through the woods behind Nettie's mansion, Goose met Miss Daphney, who became his best friend. Goose loves to visit her cottage, where he spends countless hours with Miss Daphney and her closest friends, Miss Potter and Mushroom. On those afternoons, Miss Daphney always serves cinnamon muffins smothered in orange marmalade. Sometimes Miss Daphney invites the whole group over to her house for tea, and then reads everyone tales of Benjamin Bunny. Goose may be shy around children, but when he is with Miss Daphney, Miss Potter and Mushroom, he acts just like the little bear cub he always wanted to be!

Gooseberry Materials
(14" Bear)

Fur
⅜ yd. short-nap red fur (you can also purchase white fur and dye it with berry juice)

Stuffing
12 oz. bag polyester stuffing

Eyes
8 mm black glass eyes

Paws
Two squares or ⅛ yd. tan wool felt, or any felt to contrast dyed fur

Joints
10 disks, 1½"-diameter
Materials for five sets of joints (See *General Instructions* for options)

Other Materials
Black embroidery floss for nose
Heavy carpet or buttonhole thread, for closing openings and sewing in eyes
Sewing thread to match fur

Tools
Awl or large needle for punching holes for joints and eyes
Basting needle
Embroidery needle
Fur-grooming brush (dog or cat brush works well)
Hot glue gun for neck joint (optional)
Mustache trimmers for trimming fur
Needle-nose pliers (optional)
Scissors
Sewing machine with heavy-duty needle
Stick pins for positioning ears
Stuffing stick or wooden spoon
Tools as required for chosen jointing system
Tracing paper and pencil for transferring pattern from book
7" to 12" needle for sewing in eyes.

Finishing

Gooseberry has the same body parts as Miss Marigold, Miss Pansy and Norman, but his head is different. Use the head pattern on page 51 and the body patterns on pages 31–33. Begin by reading the *General Instructions* on pages 19–25. Follow the *General Instructions* for sewing and assembly. Trim nose according to photograph. Gooseberry's nose can also be left untrimmed, as the fur nap is short.

For a Christmas Gooseberry, use red & green plaid wool for the paws and add a plaid bow tie. Gooseberry loves Christmas, because that is the day he was adopted by Nettie. He was happy to be adopted by her, but he only got one hug from her that day, and not too many after that. Nettie has since grown up, but Gooseberry receives a lot of hugs from Nettie's children. Nettie tells her children that Gooseberry needs to get extra hugs, because she did not give him enough when she was their age. Gooseberry agrees, but he still likes to hide whenever the children get too noisy.

Teddy Bear Tips

Clothing from the early 1900s works beautifully for Teddy Bears. A little bear can be very charming in blue denim coveralls and a red handkerchief in its back pocket.

You can easily make your own clothing for your bear by using baby patterns. For an 18" bear, you would use a newborn size.

Gooseberry still has a habit of taking long naps in clever hiding places. One time, the maid found him napping in the flour bin. She screamed and ran because she thought he was a little ghost!

Miss Potter, Miss Daphney's closest friend of all! See page 29 for finishing information.

Mushroom's personality makes up for his lack of fur. See page 37 for finishing information.

Miss Potter and Mushroom wait patiently for Miss Daphney to serve tea.

Miss Potter is proud of her "inexpensive" fur coat–especially when Mushroom is made of felt.

Rosie and Gooseberry on the Valentine's Day Swing

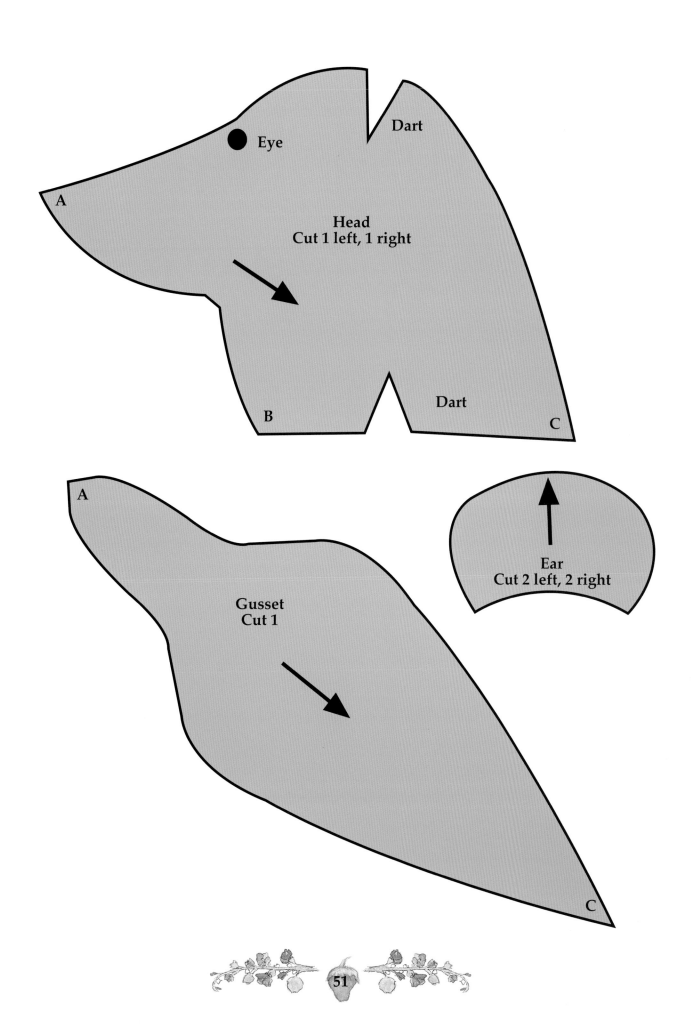

Eye

Dart

A

Head
Cut 1 left, 1 right

B

Dart

C

A

Gusset
Cut 1

Ear
Cut 2 left, 2 right

C

Miss Ivy Meadowsweet

Miss Ivy Meadowsweet can usually be found in her garden, daydreaming in a white wicker chair.

She always has a pot of fresh mint tea set on a table beside her, just in case guests wish to drop in. Miss Ivy's friends love to be invited for tea in her garden, where only strictly proper behavior is allowed. Miss Ivy dresses for tea in her finest clothing, no matter how hot the weather is. She always takes utmost care not to spill her tea on her pretty dresses of embroidered linen or antique lace that are always draped just so over layers and layers of lacy petticoats.

She always carries a lace parasol to protect herself from the sun. Years have past since her friends last reminded Miss Ivy that bears cannot get a sunburn.

She is anticipating a visit today from a very old friend, Phillepe, who is travelling all the way from Venice. Phillepe is a very famous impressionist painter, and Miss Ivy is proud of his numerous paintings featured in her parlor.

Note the personality in Miss Ivy's face–such effect comes from spending extra time experiment-ing with eye placement, ear place-ment, and trimming the snout

A rare glimpse of Miss Ivy without her "garden wear"

Miss Ivy Meadowsweet Materials
(20" Bear)

Fur
½ yd. vintage finish mohair

Stuffing
Two 12 oz. bags polyester stuffing

Eyes
12 mm black glass eyes

Paws
Two squares or ⅛ yd. tan wool felt

Joints
10 disks, 2½"-diameter
Materials for five sets of joints (See *General Instructions* for options)

Other Materials
Black embroidery floss for nose
Heavy carpet or buttonhole thread, for closing openings and sewing in eyes
Sewing thread to match fur

Tools
Awl or large needle for punching holes for joints and eyes
Basting needle
Embroidery needle
Fur-grooming brush (dog or cat brush works well)
Hot glue gun for neck joint (optional)
Mustache trimmers for trimming fur
Needle-nose pliers (optional)
Scissors
Sewing machine with heavy-duty needle
Stick pins for positioning ears
Stuffing stick or wooden spoon
Tools as required for chosen jointing system
Tracing paper and pencil for transferring pattern from book
7" to 12" needle for sewing in eyes.

Finishing

Begin by reading the *General Instructions* on pages 19–25. Cut fur according to patterns on pages 57–63. Follow the *General Instructions* for sewing and assembly. Trim nose according to photograph.

I shopped in antique shops for Miss Ivy's lovely clothes. I also found an antique parasol for her. She is wearing early 1900s baby clothing. Look for clothing in a used-clothing store or thrift store, or perhaps use a special dress from your family. Antique Christening gowns make a perfect dress for a bear of this size. Let the dress hang long and drape down past her feet.

Miss Ivy would look wonderful on your bed, and in fact prefers to stay on your bed as much as possible. During the winter, when larger varieties of bears hibernate, she frequently only sleeps in past breakfast. When this happens, be sure to wake her in time for tea, or she'll be sluggish the rest of the day. She would be grateful if you double the portions on the days she does sleep in; even when hungry, Miss Ivy is too polite to ask for second helpings.

Teddy Bear Tips

Visit flea markets and garage sales for wonderful bear accessories. You might even find an antique white dress. If a dress is discolored, brighten it with a non-chlorine whitener.

If the dress is very delicate (it feels brittle), I would hesitate to wash it. However, if there is no alternative, try carefully washing it in Ivory Snow Flakes. Always rinse thoroughly. **Never put an antique in the washing machine or dryer.** Hang the dress to dry over a shower-curtain rod, or lay it flat on a towel. Never store an old dress with starch it in, or it will attract insects.

Miss Ivy has not spent an afternoon in her garden or left her home without a parasol for several years. As a result, her smooth fur is the envy of the other lady bears.

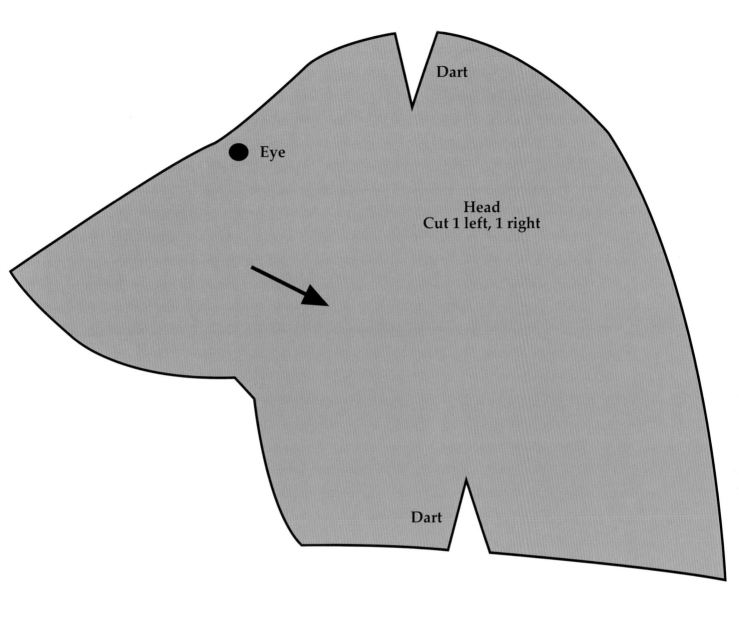

Dart

● Eye

Head
Cut 1 left, 1 right

Dart

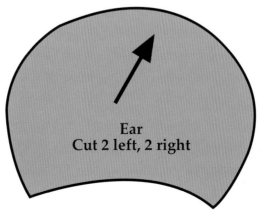

Ear
Cut 2 left, 2 right

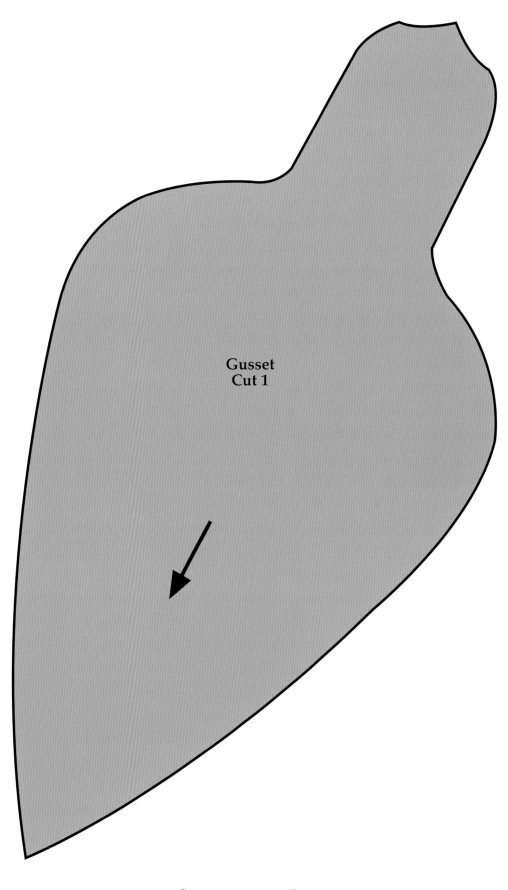

Gusset
Cut 1

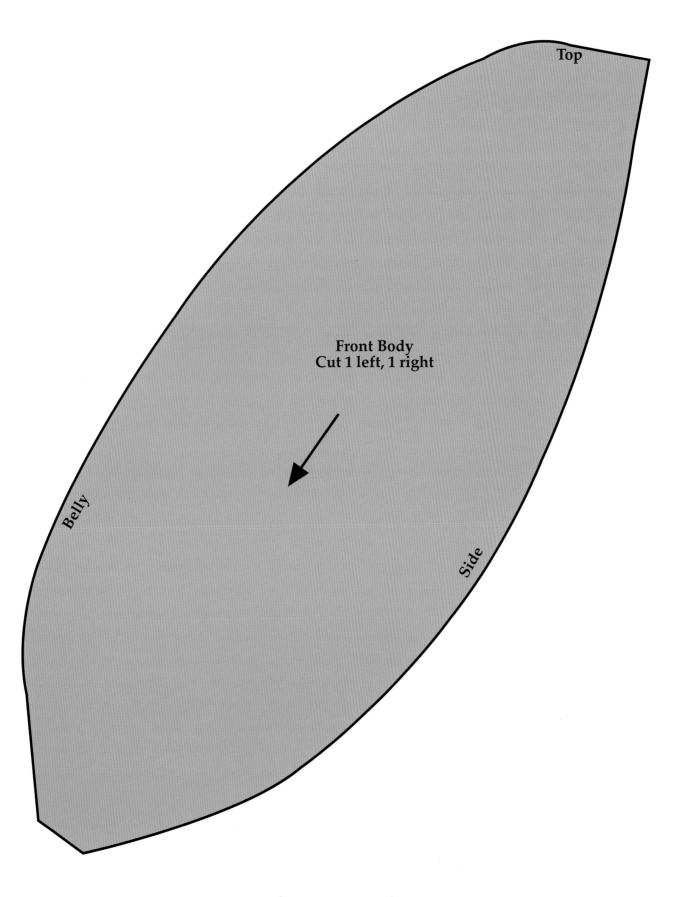

Front Body
Cut 1 left, 1 right

Top

Belly

Side

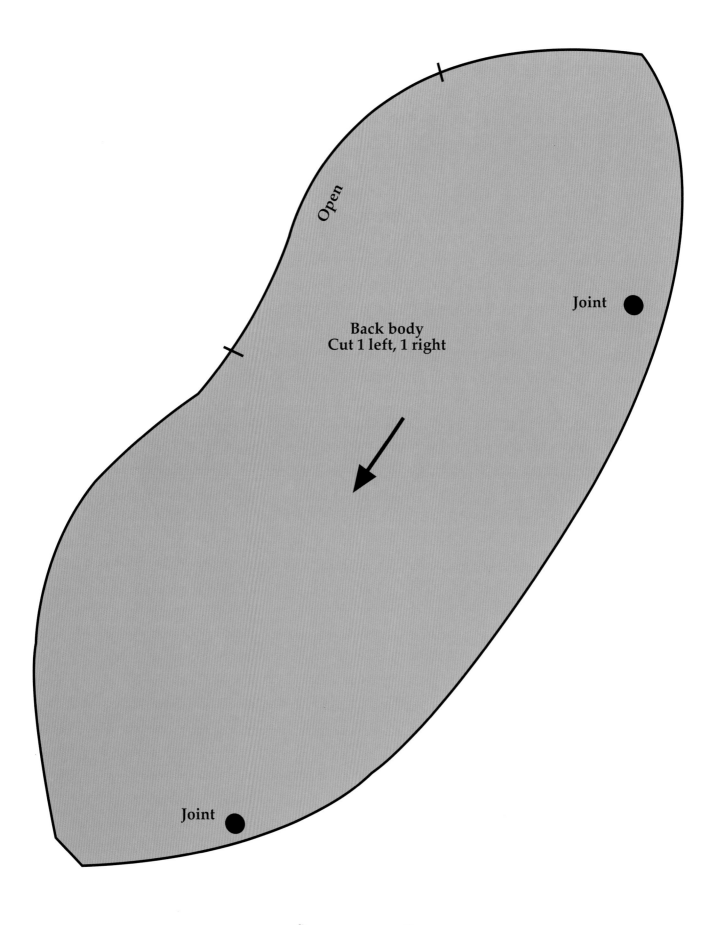

Open

Joint

Back body
Cut 1 left, 1 right

Joint

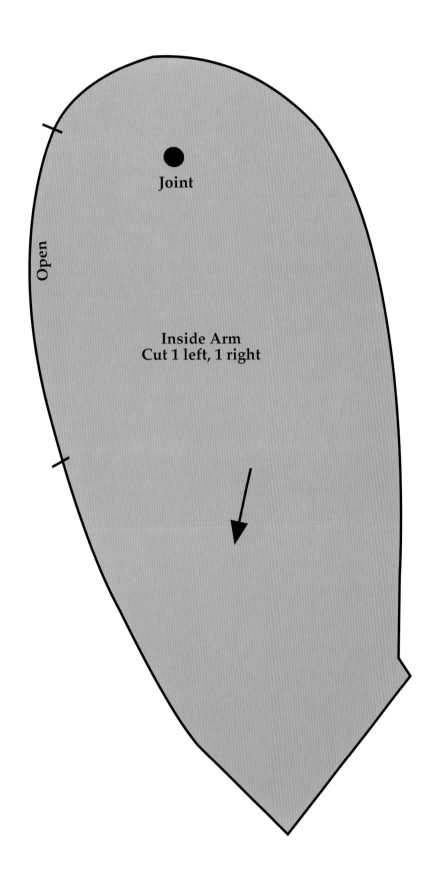

Joint

Open

Inside Arm
Cut 1 left, 1 right

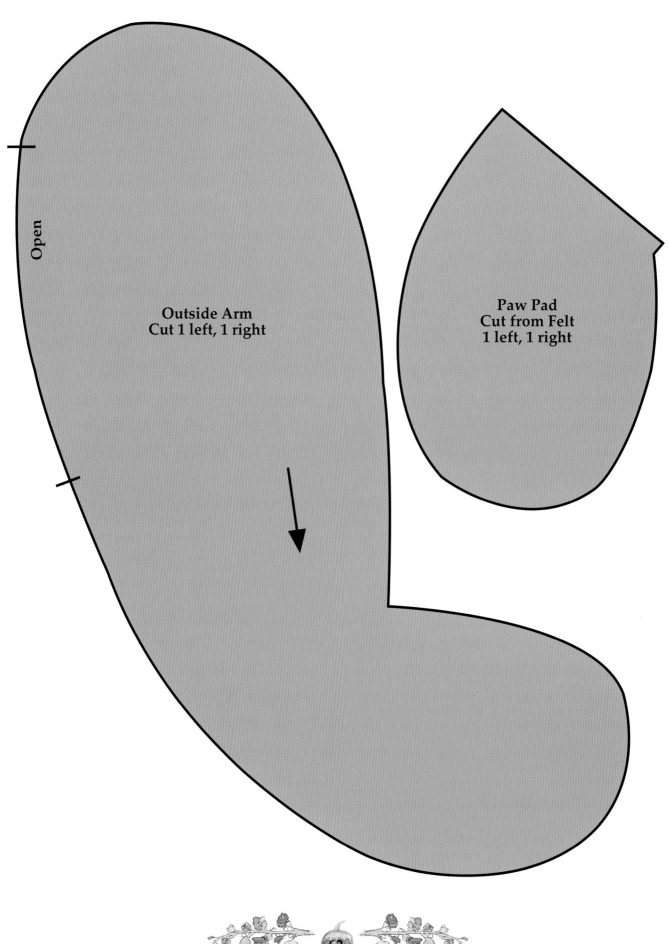

Open

Outside Arm
Cut 1 left, 1 right

Paw Pad
Cut from Felt
1 left, 1 right

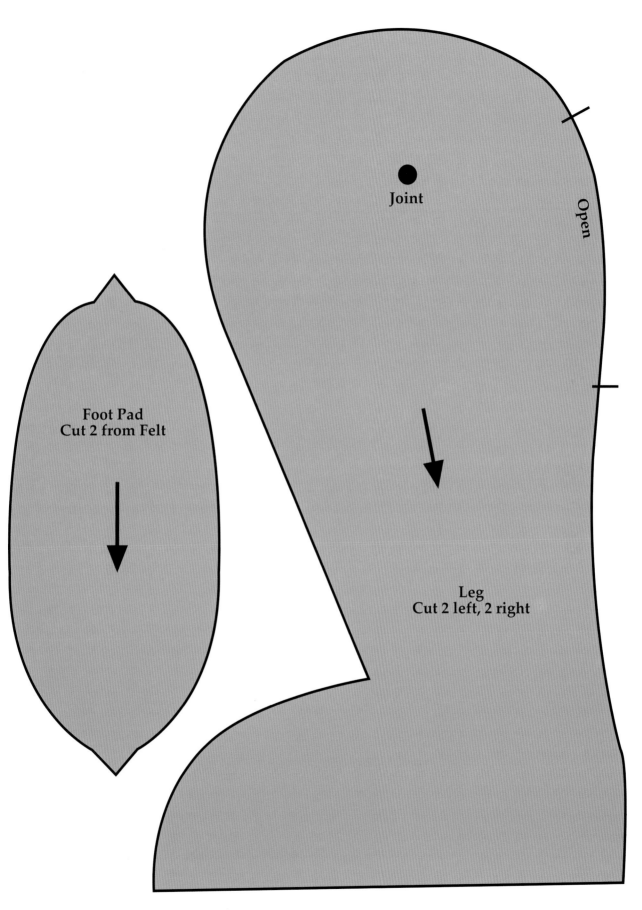

Foot Pad
Cut 2 from Felt

Joint

Open

Leg
Cut 2 left, 2 right

MISS HOLLY

Miss Holly lives near the ocean in a cozy country cottage nestled quietly at the base of a huge oak tree.

Although she receives many invitations to Teddy Bear tea parties, she rarely accepts. She is uncomfortable because she has very long silky ears unlike the round, perky ears of the other Teddy Bears. She, also, has very large eyes and a cute little nose, while all of the other Teddy Bears have long snouts and humps on their backs. She would very much like to look like the others–she so hates being different!

As a result, Miss Holly is both reclusive and introspective, and likes to spend her time reading poetry in a lacy hammock that hangs just so between two large cyprus trees, giving her a perfect view of the ocean. She is really quite a delightful bear / bunny, but few others than her family and closest friends know her well enough to understand.

Twilight is her favorite time of day, when she dances in the meadow looking for herbs and wild flowers for her basket. She takes these flowers to her Aunt Agnes, who lives a few tree trunks away. Aunt Agnes frequently assures Miss Holly that beauty is truly in the eye of the beholder!

Miss Holly has tea with Aunt Agnes and a beautiful antique doll

Miss Holly Materials
(20" Bear)

Fur
½ yd. of 1" straight long tan mohair (synthetic or plush fur works just as well)

Stuffing
Two 12 oz. bags polyester stuffing

Eyes
14 mm brown glass eyes with black pupils

Paws
Two squares or ⅛ yd. tan wool felt

Joints
10 disks, 2½"-diameter
Materials for five sets of joints (See *General Instructions* for options)

Other Materials
Brown embroidery floss for nose (pink floss may also be used)
Heavy carpet thread or buttonhole thread, for closing openings and sewing in eyes
Sewing thread to match fur

Tools
Awl or large needle for punching holes for joints and eyes
Basting needle
Embroidery needle
Fur-grooming brush (dog or cat brush works well)
Hot glue gun for neck joint (optional)
Mustache trimmers for trimming fur
Needle-nose pliers (optional)
Scissors
Sewing machine with heavy-duty needle
Stick pins for positioning ears
Stuffing stick or wooden spoon
Tools as required for chosen jointing system
Tracing paper and pencil for transferring pattern from book
7" to 12" needle for sewing in eyes.

Finishing

Except for her big feet and long ears, Miss Holly is very similar to all the other bears. Begin by reading the *General Instructions* on pages 19–25. Cut fur according to patterns on pages 69–73. Follow the *General Instructions* for sewing and assembly. Trim nose according to photograph. Her long ears are assembled the same as bear ears. Leave an opening on the side of the ear for turning; then stitch it closed with a ladder stitch. You can line the inside of the ears with felt if you wish.

I found Miss Holly's pretty dress in an antique shop in New Hampshire. Her lovely hat was purchased from a designer catalogue. You can make your own hat by purchasing a straw hat at a crafts store and gluing on silk or dried flowers. Tie pretty ribbons under her chin and she is ready for a party! Miss Holly likes to wear hats because they accentuate her pretty, long ears. She checked her genealogy and found she is a distant relative of both the Easter Bunny and Smokey the Bear. Or at least that's what she told Miss Ivy at her last party!

Teddy Bear Tips

Measure Teddy's waist and cut the length of fabric according to the fullness you wish for the skirt; then add a waistband. Old buttons finish your skirt off. Add some lace at the hem.

The inside of the ear can be made of felt or fabric, instead of using fur on both sides.

Miss Holly still dances in the meadow at twilight, but now she has a bear friend, Miss Sunflower. Almost every evening is spent chatting and gathering herbs and wild flowers until it is too dark to see.

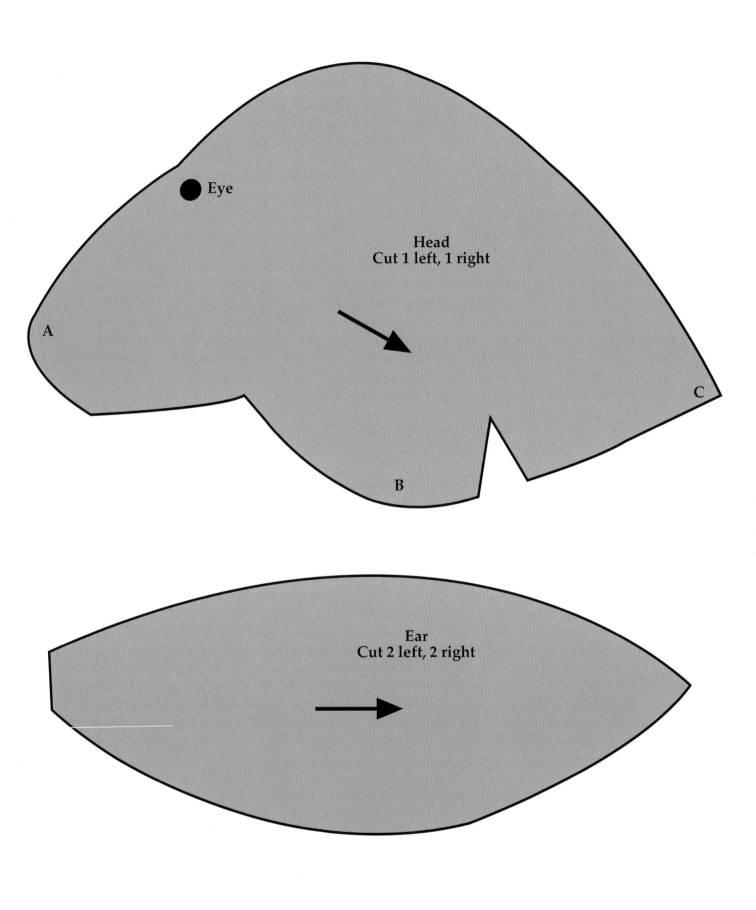

Eye

Head
Cut 1 left, 1 right

A

B

C

Ear
Cut 2 left, 2 right

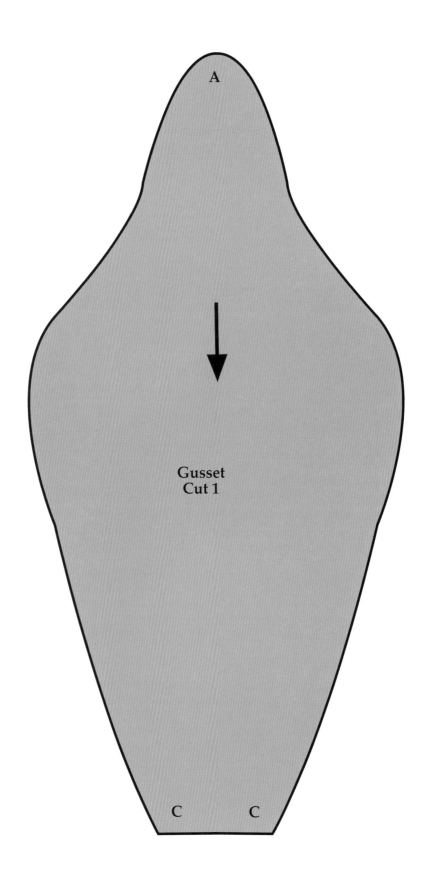

A

Gusset
Cut 1

C   C

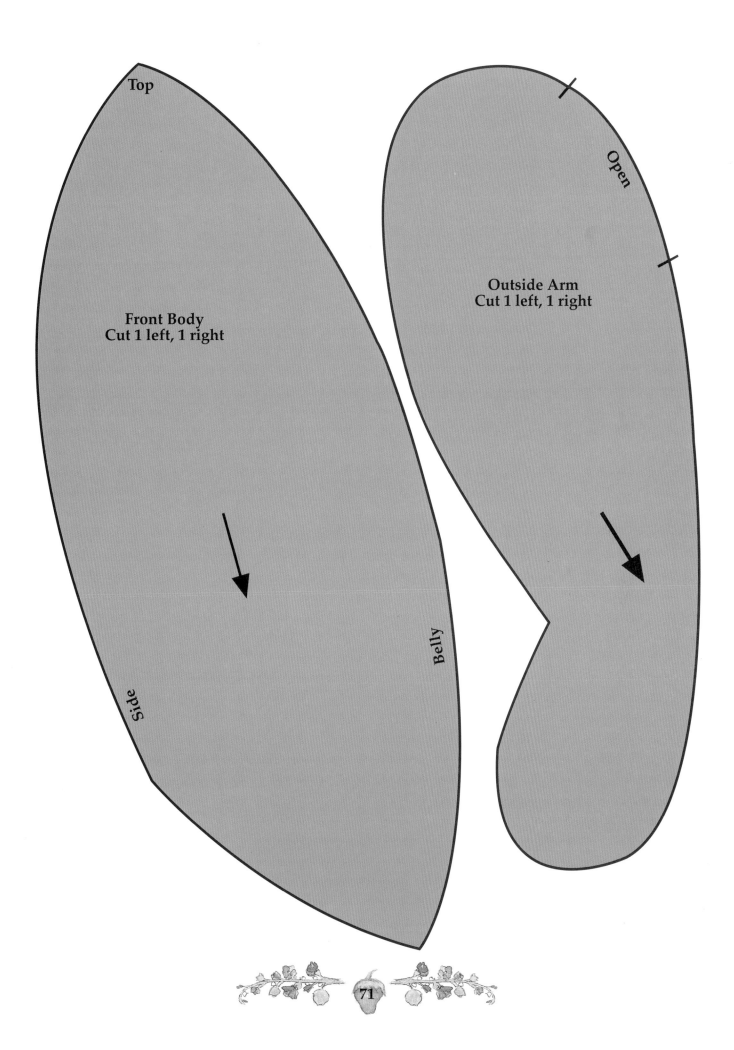

Top

Front Body
Cut 1 left, 1 right

Side

Belly

Open

Outside Arm
Cut 1 left, 1 right

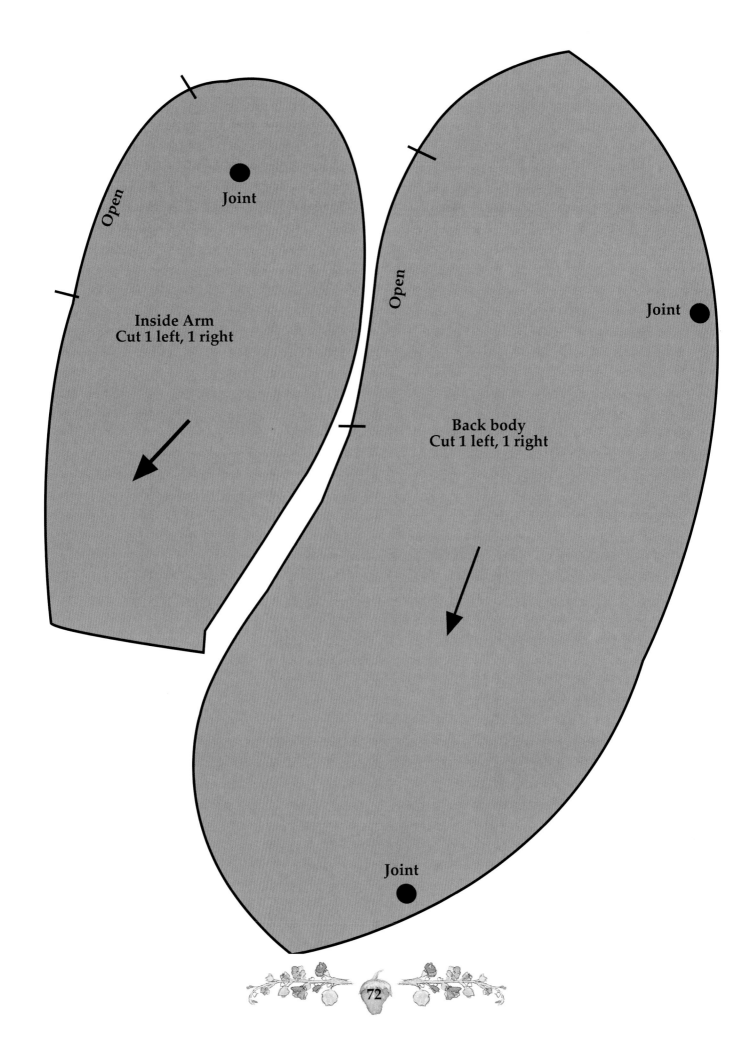

Inside Arm
Cut 1 left, 1 right

Open

Joint

Back body
Cut 1 left, 1 right

Open

Joint

Joint

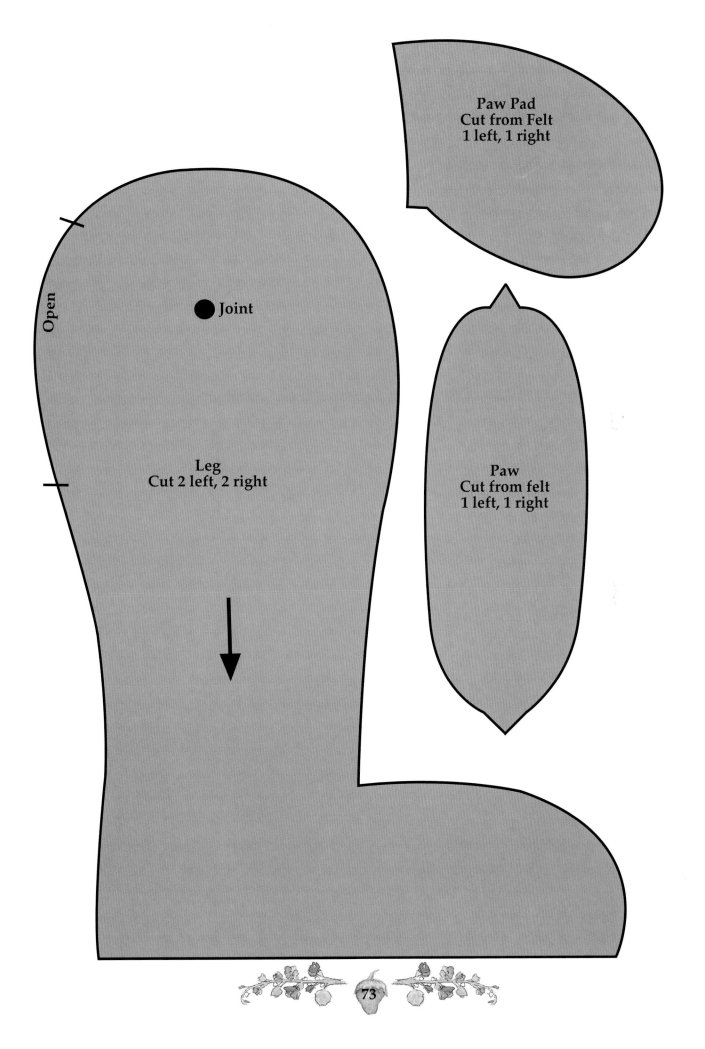

Paw Pad
Cut from Felt
1 left, 1 right

Open

● Joint

Leg
Cut 2 left, 2 right

Paw
Cut from felt
1 left, 1 right

Miss Annebelle

Miss Annebelle is probably the sweetest bear you will ever meet. She is always happy, and always has time to help Webster in his garden.

Unfortunately, she also loves pretty clothes and parasols. The combination of working in the garden and pretty clothes often creates quite a bit of extra work.

But not only is Miss Annebelle good natured about garden work, she actually loves to do the wash. The smell of freshly ironed linens is as wonderful to her as the scent of freshly cut flowers. She gets plenty of both scents nearly every day. She also knows working with Webster in the garden keeps him from having tea with Miss Ivy, who only sits among the flowers and never gets her paws dirty. For some reason she can't quite explain, Miss Annebelle is suspicious of a bear without dirt under its claws.

Early in the morning before the day's chores have begun, Miss Annebelle enjoys sitting alone in her nightgown among the flowers from her garden, sipping her own blend of "morning tea."

(18" Bear)

Fur

½ yd. Champagne-colored curly mohair

Stuffing

Two 12 oz. bags polyester stuffing

Eyes

12 or 14 mm black glass eyes

Paws

Two squares or ⅛ yd. tan wool felt

Joints

10 disks, 2½"-diameter
Materials for five sets of joints (See *General Instructions* for options)

Other Materials

Brown embroidery floss for nose
Heavy carpet or buttonhole thread, for closing openings and sewing in eyes
Sewing thread to match fur

Tools

Awl or large needle for punching holes for joints and eyes
Basting needle
Embroidery needle
Fur-grooming brush (dog or cat brush works well)
Hot glue gun for neck joint (optional)
Mustache trimmers for trimming fur
Needle-nose pliers (optional)
Scissors
Sewing machine with heavy-duty needle
Stick pins for positioning ears
Stuffing stick or wooden spoon
Tools as required for chosen jointing system
Tracing paper and pencil for transferring pattern from book
7" to 12" needle for sewing in eyes.

Begin by reading the *General Instructions* on pages 19–25. Cut fur according to patterns on pages 84–89. Follow the *General Instructions* for sewing and assembly. Trim nose according to photograph. Notice Annebelle's nose embroidery is different from Webster's, giving her a definitely feminine look.

I found Annebelle's dress in an antique shop. It is a little large for her, but it really looks very cute that way. Any excess fabric can be caught up with a ribbon, which makes Annebelle look like she is playing dress-up in the attic. A ribbon bow will help complete the look.

As much as she likes to dress up, Annebelle has much more fun dressing up the young cubs that come by. Patches is her most frequent and most unwilling victim. Not long ago, while Annebelle's back was turned, Patches grew weary of posing and ran outside to play without remembering to remove his clothing first. Upon discovering that her laciest gown had been soiled with grass stains and tree sap, Annebelle found someone a bit more patient.

Teddy Bear Tips

When you sit your bear in a chair, turn its head at an angle and tip the nose down. It will be looking right at you, and you can almost hear a friendly growl.

Even after washing it almost every day, Miss Annebelle's clothing looks as new as the day she made it. Other bears have asked how she keeps her clothes from looking worn. Miss Annebelle always replies that sitting in a chair at tea causes more wear and tear than standing in the garden all day.

Webster

Webster is a charming, gentle fellow who lives at the edge of the village in a picturesque English-style cottage.

His days are spent working in his lovely English garden. Webster can usually be seen among the bushes or somewhere along the path in his ever-present bow tie cultivating or trimming his heirloom old-world roses. He is very proud of his high-topped leather shoes with miniature wooden buttons–even though buttoning those shoes is a frustrating process for someone with chubby paws like Webster!

He feels it is most important to dress correctly while tending to his garden. After all, Webster loves the company of Miss Annebelle as much as he loves his garden. Every afternoon at tea time, he carries a large bouquet freshly picked from his garden and goes to visit Miss Annebelle. They oftentimes sit for hours drinking jasmine tea and chatting the afternoon away.

One rainy night, after a day when Webster had missed both working in his garden and having tea with Miss Annebelle, he had a disturbing dream: he was a butler in a large English Manor who was locked outside in the rain and could not find his key to either the front door or the gardening shed. Upon awakening, he discovered the key in his chubby paw, but could not remember where the Manor was. He now keeps his boots on and the key hung on a ribbon around his neck–just in case he has the dream again!

Miss
Annebelle
has her
morning
tea while
she waits
for
Webster's
arrival

Webster joins the ladies for afternoon tea

Miss Annebelle and Webster's wedding photo

Webster Materials
(18" bear)

Fur
½ yd. vintage finish mohair

Stuffing
6 oz. polyester plus 12 oz. excelsior stuffing (combined for a wonderful "old" feel and look)
Optional Stuffing:
Two 12 oz. bags of polyester filling

Eyes
12 mm black glass eyes

Paws
Two squares or ⅛ yd. tan wool felt

Joints
10 disks, 2½" diameter
Materials for five sets of joints (See *General Instructions* for options)

Other Materials
Black embroidery floss for nose
Heavy carpet or buttonhole thread, for closing openings and sewing in eyes
Sewing thread to match fur

Tools
Awl or large needle for punching holes for joints and eyes
Basting needle
Embroidery needle
Fur-grooming brush (dog or cat brush works well)
Hot glue gun for neck joint (optional)
Mustache trimmers for trimming fur
Needle-nose pliers (optional)
Scissors
Sewing machine with heavy-duty needle
Stick pins for positioning ears
Stuffing stick or wooden spoon
Tools as required for chosen jointing system
Tracing paper and pencil for transferring pattern from book
7" to 12" needle for sewing in eyes.

Begin by reading the *General Instructions* on pages 19–25. Cut fur according to patterns on pages 84–89. Follow the *General Instructions* for sewing and assembly. Trim nose according to photograph. Notice that Webster's nose embroidery is distinctly different from the other bears. I suggest cutting a piece of black felt for a template, and basting it to the nose, then embroidering over the template. If you are like me, you may find yourself needing to re-embroider the nose several times before it looks just right. If this is the case, cut across the threads, pull them out with needle-nose pliers and restitch.

**Webster's nose
(not actual size)**

To make Webster's antique shoes fit, I inserted the sewn leg into the shoe and then stuffed the foot while it was inside the shoe. If you don't do this, his foot might be too fat to fit into the shoe. Because I did this, I can even remove his shoes and put them back on easily. I stuffed the head and paws firmly with stuffing and filled the body and tops of arms and legs loosely with excelsior.

When Webster was assembled, I cut tiny holes in his paws and brushed the edges for a worn look. (Do not brush too much, as you will ruin the antiquing.) Then I gave him a tea bath (made with a cup of tea of any flavor, cooled. I like to drink a cup while I wait for the tea to cool). Apply the tea with a sponge (Webster likes this part because it tickles). Sponge the brushed-paw areas as well. Let him play outside to dry. If he climbs a tree and gets dirty, that's okay. He'll just look more antiqued. I found Webster's shoes and key at an antique flea market.

Teddy Bear Tips

Sit a Teddy Bear near the door and let him wear your sunglasses or reading glasses when you are not using them. You can also always trust him with your keys. I guarantee you will always be able to find them if Teddy is there to keep track of them!

Even though Webster has learned to unbutton his shoes, he still wears them to bed. He is not lazy, but if he ever has his dream again, he needs to be wearing his boots, just in case it is raining in his dream.

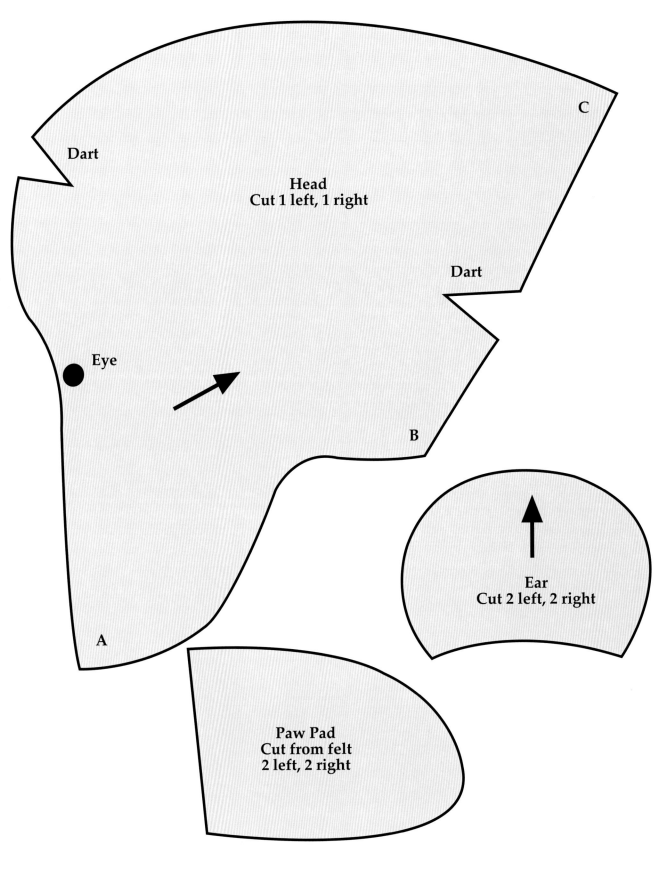

Dart

Head
Cut 1 left, 1 right

C

Dart

Eye

B

A

Ear
Cut 2 left, 2 right

Paw Pad
Cut from felt
2 left, 2 right

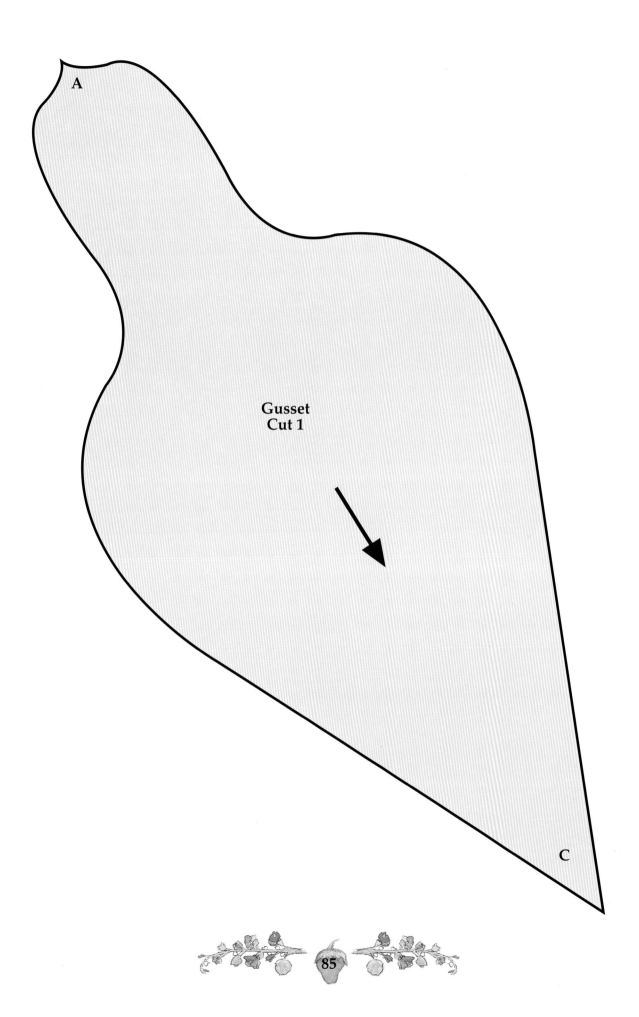

Gusset
Cut 1

A

C

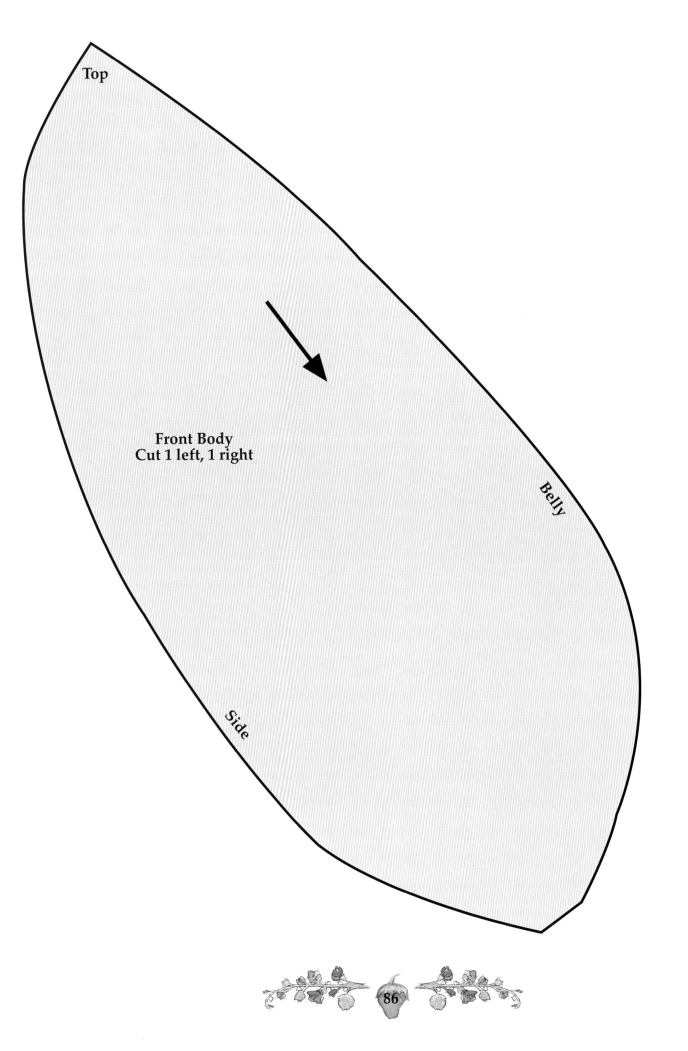

Top

Front Body
Cut 1 left, 1 right

Belly

Side

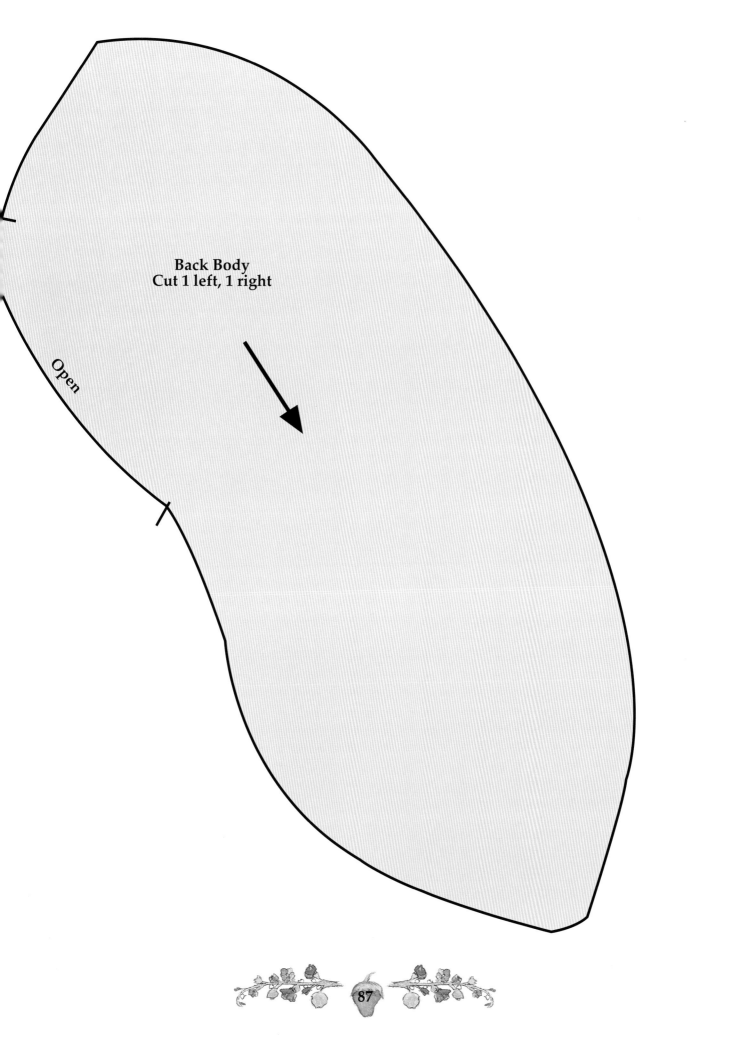

Back Body
Cut 1 left, 1 right

Open

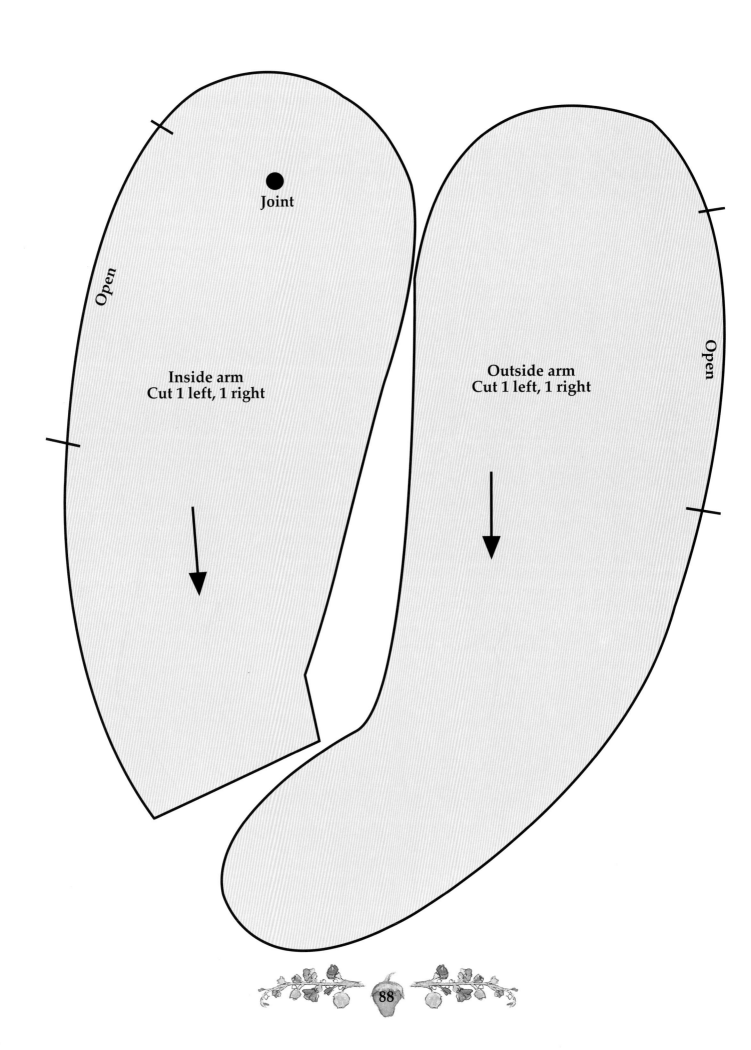

Joint

Open

Inside arm
Cut 1 left, 1 right

Outside arm
Cut 1 left, 1 right

Open

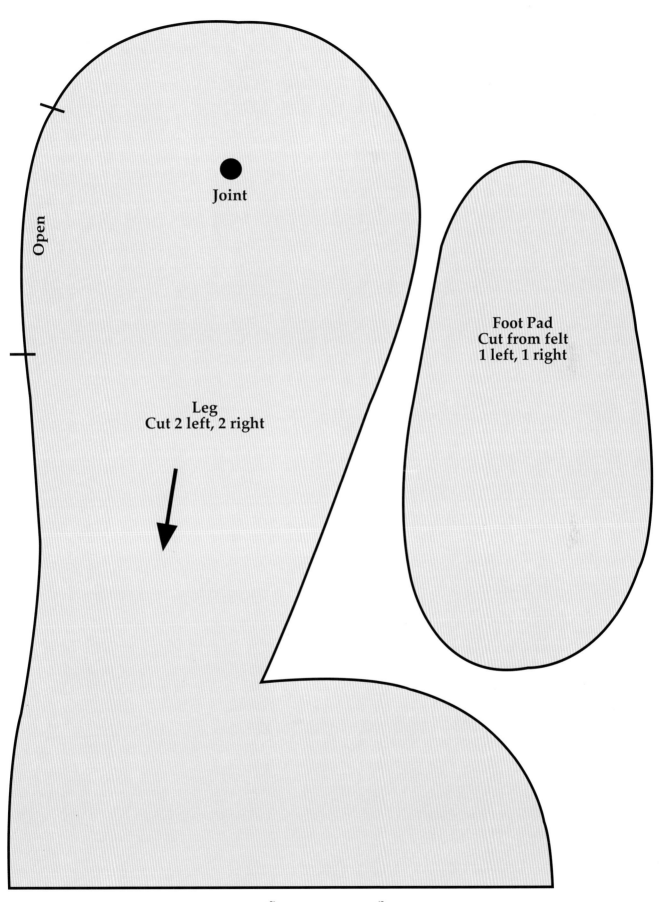

Joint

Open

Leg
Cut 2 left, 2 right

Foot Pad
Cut from felt
1 left, 1 right

Miss Emily

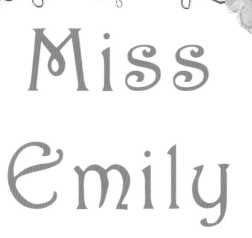

Miss Emily loves to play the violin and sees herself as very musically blessed. She claims to be a genius who never needed formal training.

According to Miss Emily, she played a beautiful song the first time she picked up her violin. Her friends agree that the song was beautiful, but after hearing her perform it so many times, they wish she would learn another one.

Despite her high opinion of her own musicianship, Miss Emily is really a very kind, loving bear. She is always happy, and brightens the spirits of the other bears because she sings everywhere she goes.

Although she really cannot sing any better than any of the other bears, her voice is even more popular than her violin playing because she can sing more than one song.

Miss Emily loves to listen to Bach and Vivaldi, and occasionally puts on a pretty batiste dress and carriage coat for a trip to see the symphony. A friend recently helped her fill out an audition form for the symphony, and Miss Emily dreams that one day she will be "first violin."

Miss Emily poses with a bouquet from an anonymous fan

Miss Emily Materials
(15" Bear)

Fur
½ yd. Merino wool or other short-nap fur

Stuffing
Two 12 oz. bags polyester stuffing

Eyes
12 mm brown safety eyes with black pupils

Paws
Two squares or ⅛ yd. of tan wool felt

Joints
10 disks, 2½"-diameter
Materials for five sets of joints (See *General Instructions* for options)

Other Materials
Black embroidery floss for nose
Heavy carpet or buttonhole thread, for closing openings and sewing in eyes
Sewing thread to match fur

Tools
Awl or large needle for punching holes for joints and eyes
Basting needle
Embroidery needle
Fur-grooming brush (dog or cat brush works well)
Hot glue gun for neck joint (optional)
Mustache trimmers for trimming fur
Needle-nose pliers (optional)
Scissors
Sewing machine with heavy-duty needle
Stick pins for positioning ears
Stuffing stick or wooden spoon
Tools as required for chosen jointing system
Tracing paper and pencil for transferring pattern from book
7" to 12" needle for sewing in eyes.

Finishing

Begin by reading the *General Instructions* on pages 19–25. Cut fur according to patterns on pages 95–99. Follow the *General Instructions* for sewing and assembly. Notice that because of the length and style of fur, Miss Emily requires little finishing work.

I found Emily's dress and coat in an antique store in New Hampshire. It is hand embroidered with Soutash braid. In the early 1900s, all children wore these carriage coats to protect their clothing from the mud and dust that could easily get into open carriages. Her violin is actually a tiny functioning music box.

Miss Emily's recent audition with the Utah Symphony was cut short when she discovered that most violins do not have a wind-up key. It was a disappointing moment in her career, but since she was in town anyway, Miss Emily submitted an application to the Utah Opera Company. Her new ambition is to be an opera soprano. Friends of Miss Emily remind her that with her low bear voice, she will have a better chance of becoming an opera baritone!

Teddy Bear Tips

Buy white fur and tint it yourself with dye or tea. You can also use natural dyes such as walnuts, berries or berry soft drinks. Always practice on small pieces first.

Miss Emily now dedicates most of her free time to taking singing lessons. Even if she never becomes an opera star, the other bears enjoy her singing more now than they ever did.

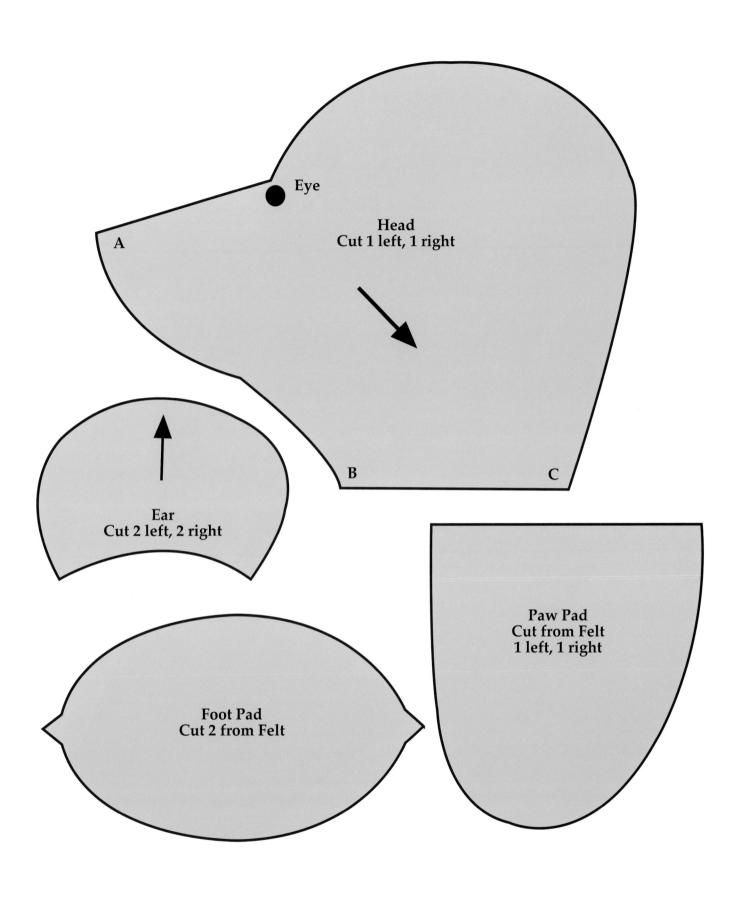

Eye

Head
Cut 1 left, 1 right

A

B   C

Ear
Cut 2 left, 2 right

Foot Pad
Cut 2 from Felt

Paw Pad
Cut from Felt
1 left, 1 right

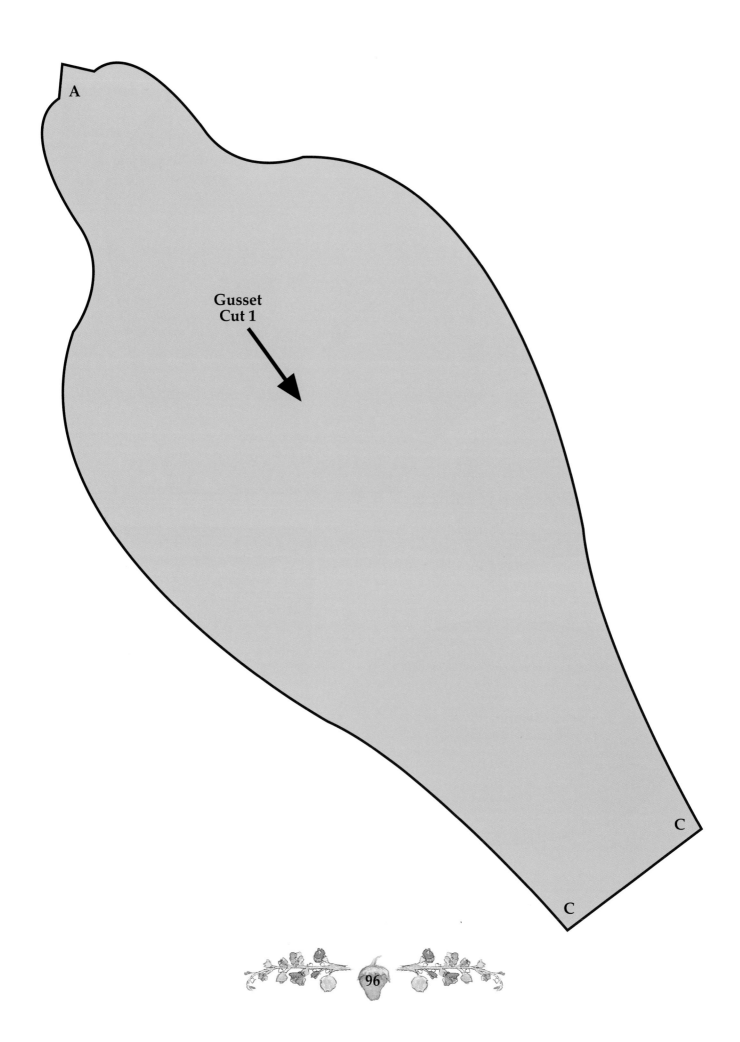

A

Gusset
Cut 1

C

C

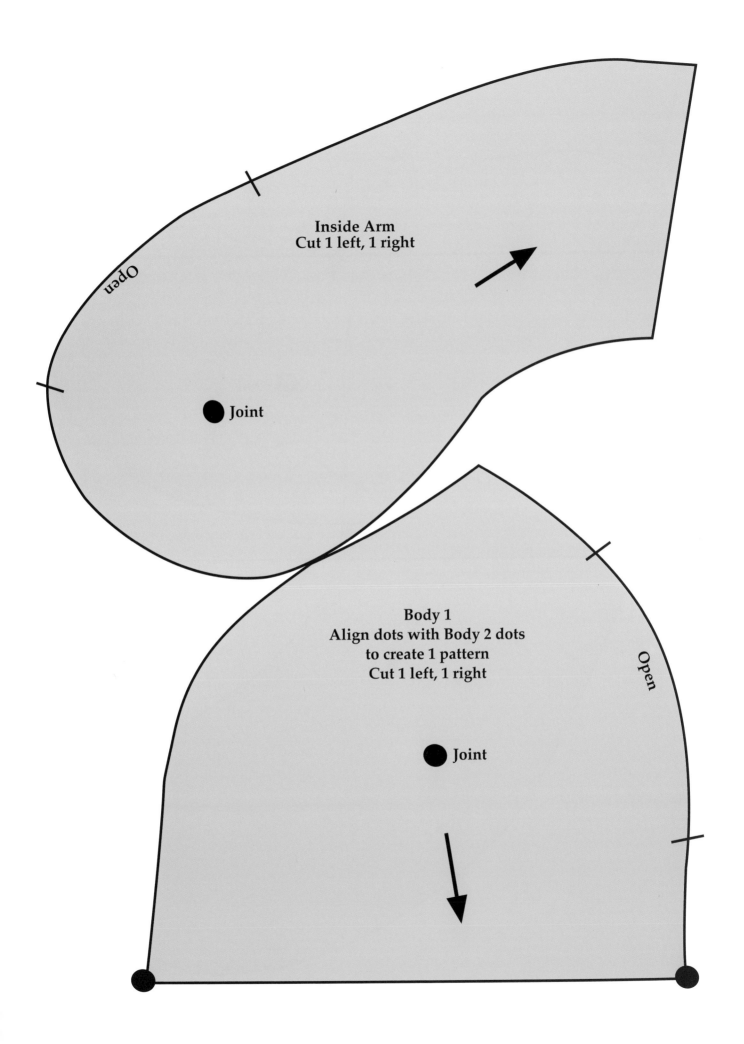

Inside Arm
Cut 1 left, 1 right

Open

● Joint

Body 1
Align dots with Body 2 dots
to create 1 pattern
Cut 1 left, 1 right

Open

● Joint

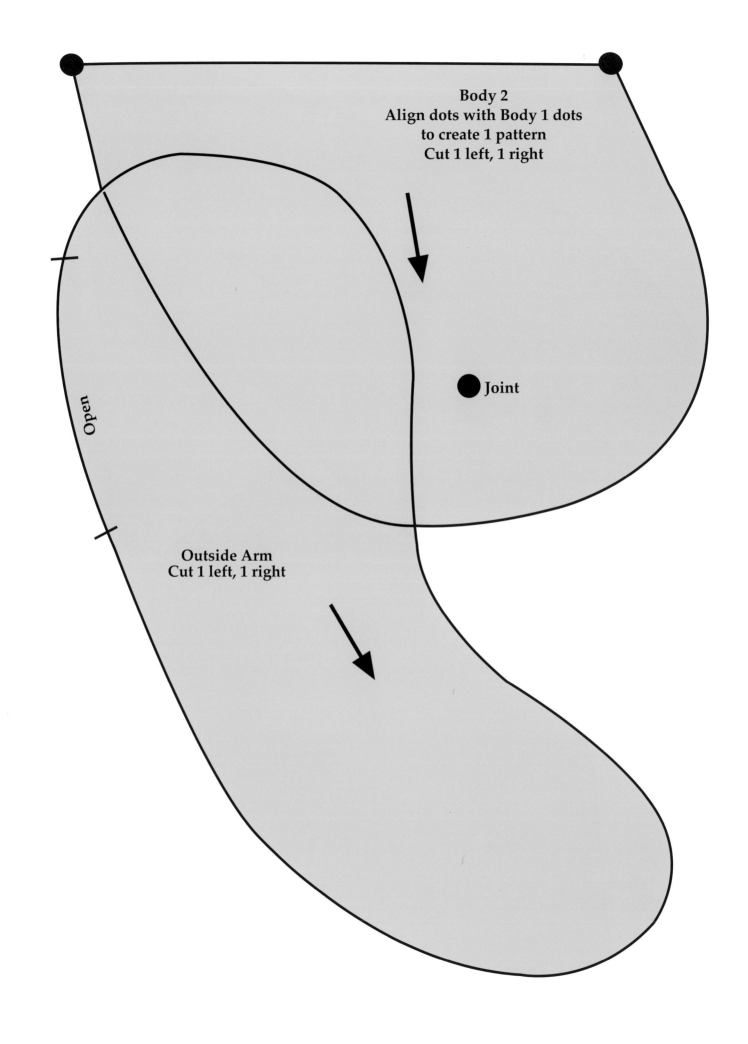

Body 2
Align dots with Body 1 dots
to create 1 pattern
Cut 1 left, 1 right

Joint

Open

Outside Arm
Cut 1 left, 1 right

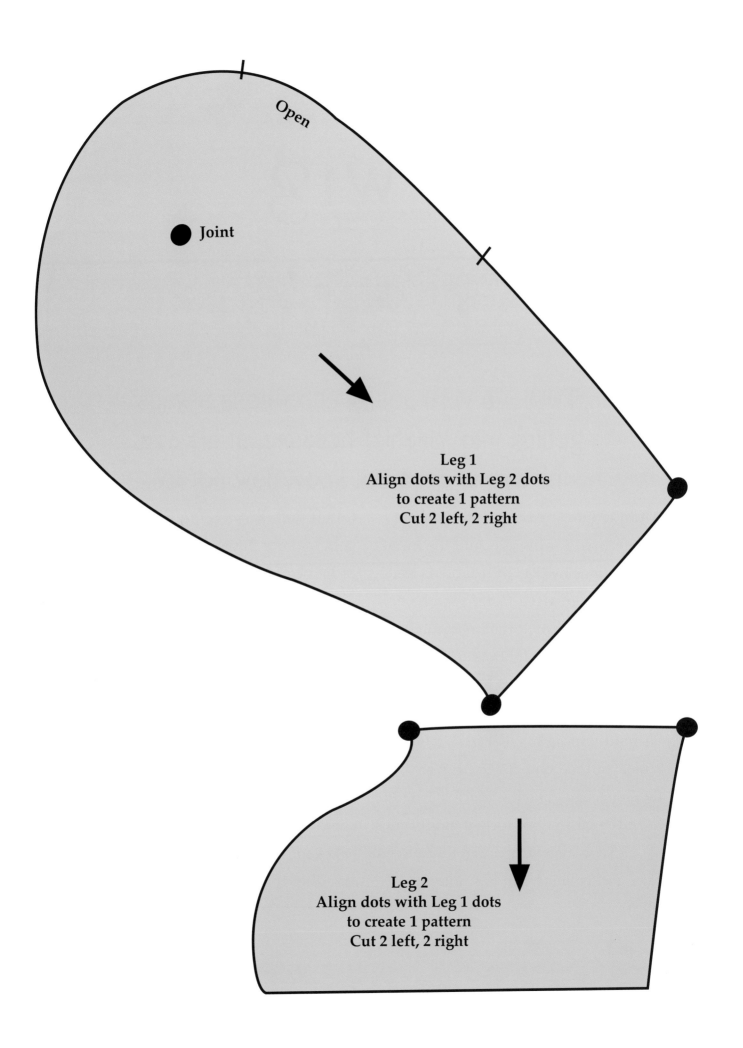

Twig

Twig is a very young cub who is always getting into mischief because, at his age, he simply does not know how not to!

Although he is young, Twig is also rather large for his age, and the number of times he gets in trouble is the only thing growing faster than he is. Twig loves to smell the honeysuckle and play in his neighbors' flower gardens and gets mud on his paws; then he runs into other people's houses without wiping his feet first. He once almost ruined one of Miss Ivy's favorite rugs. She has since learned to keep the patio door locked at all times.

Twig also very much loves to eat cake and cookies, but has not yet found that the secret to getting cookies is in leaving flower gardens and floors as he finds them.

Twig is as fast on all fours as other Teddy Bears are standing up. Although he is learning to walk upright, he prefers all fours, and his speed makes him very hard to track down. His parents have learned to follow the muddy footprints until they find him—usually at Miss Ivy's eating cookies, or at Miss Annebelle's eating cakes, or in yet another flower garden, smelling the honeysuckle.

Twig and some of his gentler friends pose for a portrait

Twig prepares to engage in his favorite activity

Twig Materials
(12" Bear)

Fur
⅜ yd. distressed short-nap mohair

Stuffing
12 oz. bag polyester stuffing

Eyes
10 mm black glass eyes

Paws
Two squares or ⅛ yd. tan wool felt

Joints
Two disks, 2½"-diameter
Materials for one joint (See *General Instructions* for options)

Other Materials
Black embroidery floss for nose
Heavy carpet or buttonhole thread, for closing openings and sewing in eyes
Sewing thread to match fur

Tools
Awl or large needle for punching holes for joints and eyes
Basting needle
Embroidery needle
Fur-grooming brush (dog or cat brush works well)
Hot glue gun for neck joint (optional)
Mustache trimmers for trimming fur
Needle-nose pliers (optional)
Scissors
Sewing machine with heavy-duty needle
Stick pins for positioning ears
Stuffing stick or wooden spoon
Tools as required for chosen jointing system
Tracing paper and pencil for transferring pattern from book
7" to 12" needle for sewing in eyes.

Finishing

Begin by reading the *General Instructions* on pages 19–25. Cut fur according to patterns on pages 106–111. Finish Twig's head according to *General Instructions*, pages 16–25.

1. Place belly pieces right sides together, and sew seam across top, according to diagram.

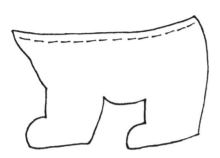

2. Pin and baste belly to back pieces, matching legs . Machine-stitch according to diagram.

3. Sew neck and back seam according to diagram.

4. Baste paw pads in place; machine-stitch. Turn bear; attach head with joint.

5. Stuff the remainder of bear. When stuffing the legs, be sure to use small pieces, stuffing them very firmly so that Twig can support himself. Mold the body as you stuff, making sure the legs are facing down, not outward.

Continue stuffing and stand him up frequently to see if he stands perfectly. Keep pushing in stuffing and adjusting the legs as you go. You can always pull out the stuffing and start again. Finish him off with a nice bow. You might also put a patchwork saddle on him or put him in a wagon with wheels.

Whatever you do, do not place Twig on a table or the kitchen counter. He is not nearly as careful as he should be, and his manners are often rather poor. He's a messy eater, and sometimes drinks straight from the tap and leaves the water running! Do not leave him alone when cookies are in the house, unless they are under lock and key!

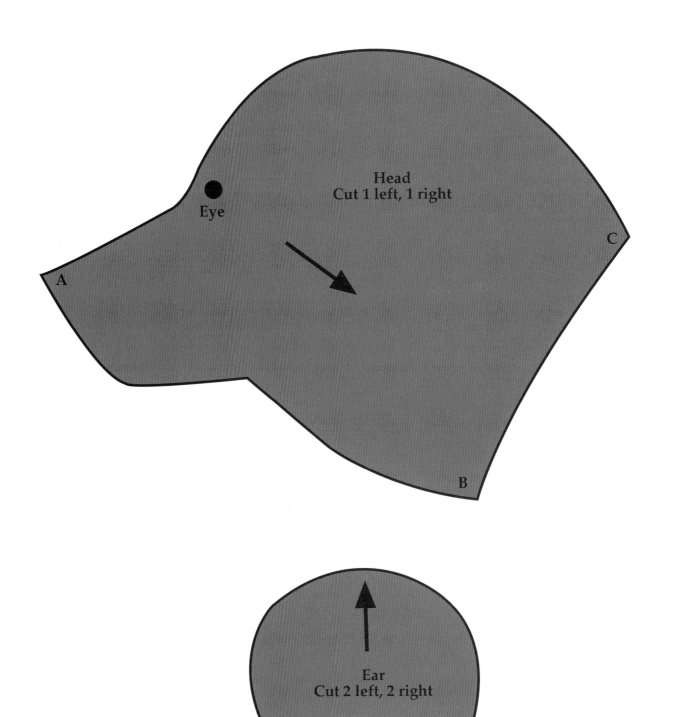

Head
Cut 1 left, 1 right

Eye

A

C

B

Ear
Cut 2 left, 2 right

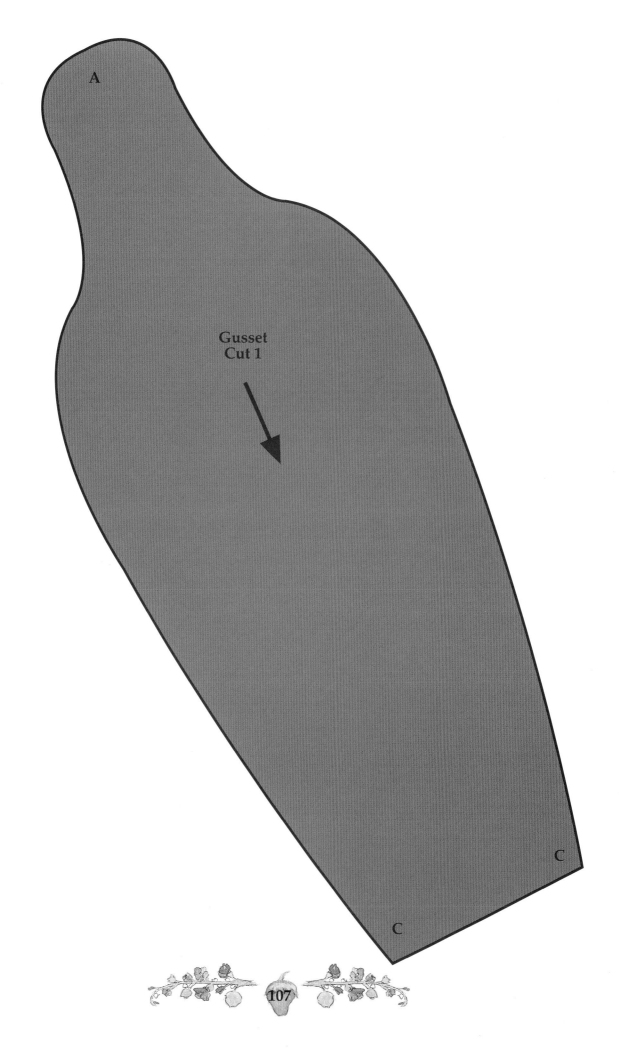

A

Gusset
Cut 1

C

C

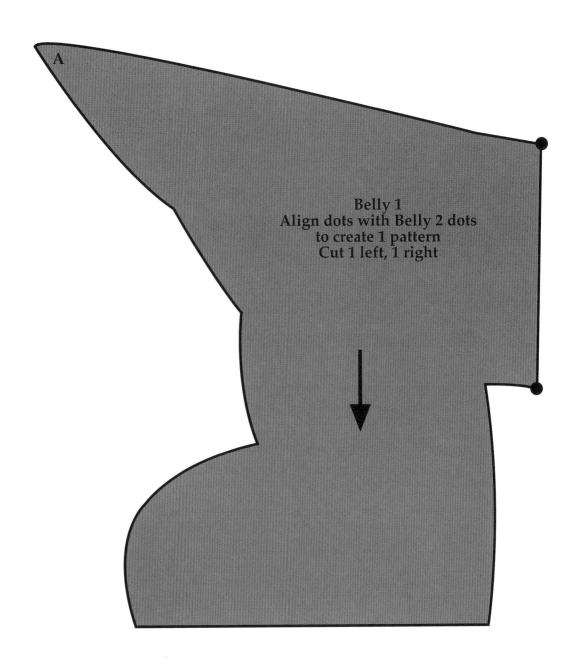

A

Belly 1
Align dots with Belly 2 dots
to create 1 pattern
Cut 1 left, 1 right

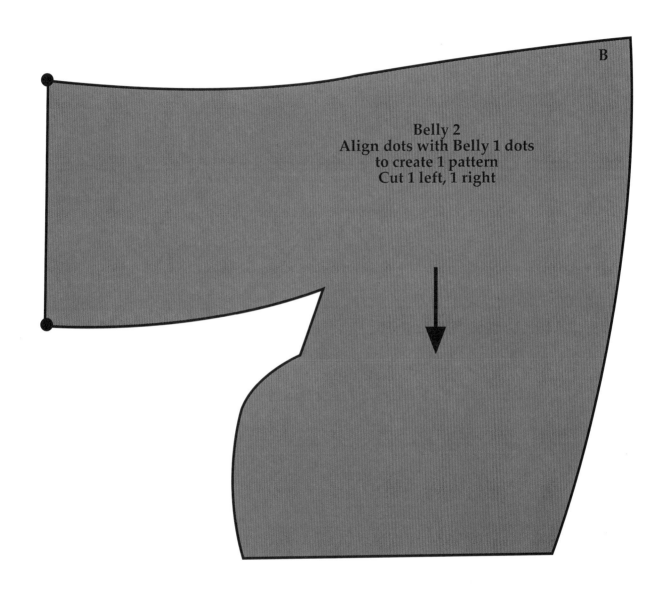

Belly 2
Align dots with Belly 1 dots
to create 1 pattern
Cut 1 left, 1 right

B

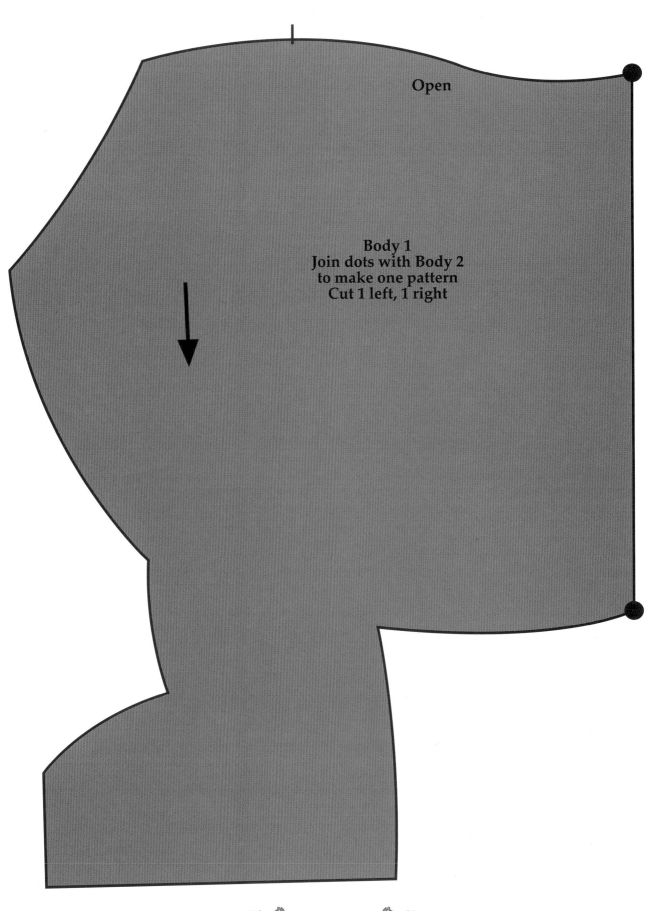

Open

Body 1
Join dots with Body 2
to make one pattern
Cut 1 left, 1 right

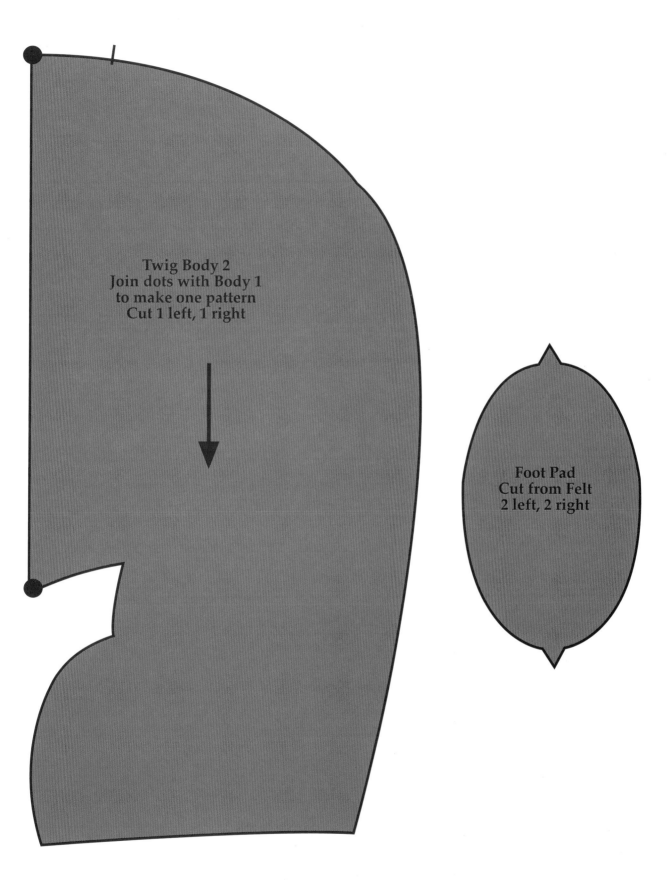

Twig Body 2
Join dots with Body 1
to make one pattern
Cut 1 left, 1 right

Foot Pad
Cut from Felt
2 left, 2 right

Patches

Patches is a little boy bear who is always getting into scraps with his playmates.

He tries very hard to get along with the other cubs, but he has such an independent mind that he has a hard time sticking to the rules of the games they are playing, especially when they have been playing a game for a long time. For example, one time they had been playing football for a while, and Patches decided he wanted to play hide and seek instead. Perhaps the other cubs would have liked the idea better if Patches had *told* them his plans before he had chosen his hiding place (or at least had not taken the ball with him). Because of his size, Patches is very good at hiding, and it took the other cubs a long time to locate him. Patches lost a bit of stuffing when they finally did find him.

The other cubs often tease Patches because his fur simply isn't as nice as theirs. This really is unkind, because Patches' mom and dad cannot afford a new coat for him every single winter. Patches doesn't mind, though. After all, he doesn't have to be as careful as the others, and nobody expects him to bathe as much.

Patches likes to visit Annebelle because she gives him Jasmine tea and honey cakes. He loves honey cakes so much that he'll even play dress-up with her. He likes wearing nice clothes sometimes, but wishes she had something other than frilly dresses to try on!

Patches sits inside his home, knowing the other cubs will not let him play football with them for a while

Patches is caught having tea with Poppy, much to his chagrin

Patches Materials
(15" Bear)

Fur
⅜ yd. short Merino wool or other short-pile fur

Stuffing
12 oz. bag polyester stuffing

Eyes
12 mm black glass eyes

Paws
Two squares or ⅛ yd. tan wool felt

Joints
10 disks, 2"-diameter
Materials for five sets of joints (See *General Instructions* for options)

Other Materials
Black embroidery floss for nose
Heavy carpet or buttonhole thread, for closing openings and sewing in eyes
Sewing thread to match fur
Scraps of material for patches

Tools
Awl or large needle for punching holes for joints and eyes
Basting needle
Embroidery needle
Fur-grooming brush (dog or cat brush works well)
Hot glue gun for neck joint (optional)
Mustache trimmers for trimming fur
Needle-nose pliers (optional)
Scissors
Sewing machine with heavy-duty needle
Stick pins for positioning ears
Stuffing stick or wooden spoon
Tools as required for chosen jointing system
Tracing paper and pencil for transferring pattern from book
7" to 12" needle for sewing in eyes.

Finishing

Patches was really fun to make, especially since his body is only two pieces instead of four. I sewed the patches on before assembling him. Begin by reading the *General Instructions* on pages 19–25. Cut fur according to the patterns on pages 117–121. I used black thread to sew scratches on his arms, legs and cheeks (see photos). To give Patches a slumped or relaxed look, do not stuff the top of his body as firmly, so that his head tilts forward.

Please note the little black stitches to the sides of his eyes that give him a sad look. They really add to his personality as a little bear whose unusually curious nature is not helped at all by his lack of coordination. Patches needs an extra patch and a gentle scolding once in a while, but mostly he needs lots and lots of hugs and extra helpings of chocolate-chip cookies or tiny honey cakes topped with fresh whipped cream.

Teddy Bear Tips

When antiquing paws and paw pads, use yarn of different colors, stitching criss-cross to make paws look like they have been repaired.

To further antique your Teddy, cut fur short in patches on the arms, belly, top of head and toes, where the bear might have received more wear and tear during a long lifetime.

When Patches gets too unruly when playing with the older cubs, they tell him they would like to play hide and seek. Patches always finds a good spot to hide, but wonders why no one ever seems to find him. In fact, no one ever seems to be looking for him, either. He usually hides for several hours before giving up and finding the older cubs playing football. They tell Patches he is just too good at hiding, but he is beginning to become suspicious!

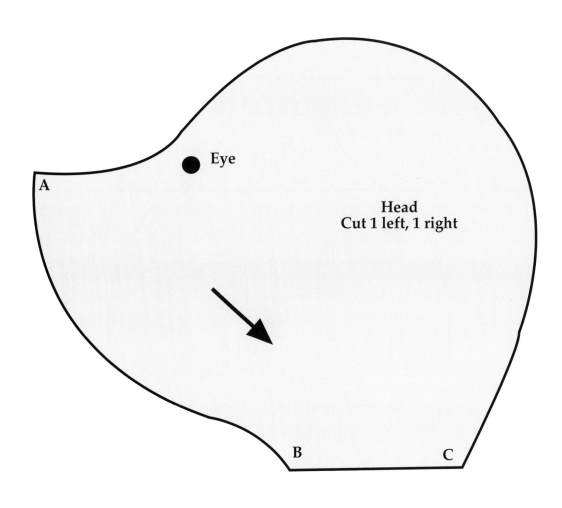

Eye

A

**Head
Cut 1 left, 1 right**

B   C

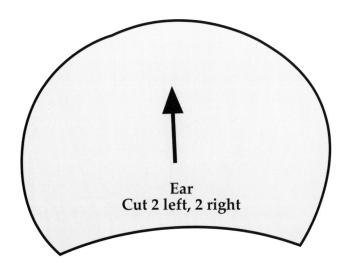

**Ear
Cut 2 left, 2 right**

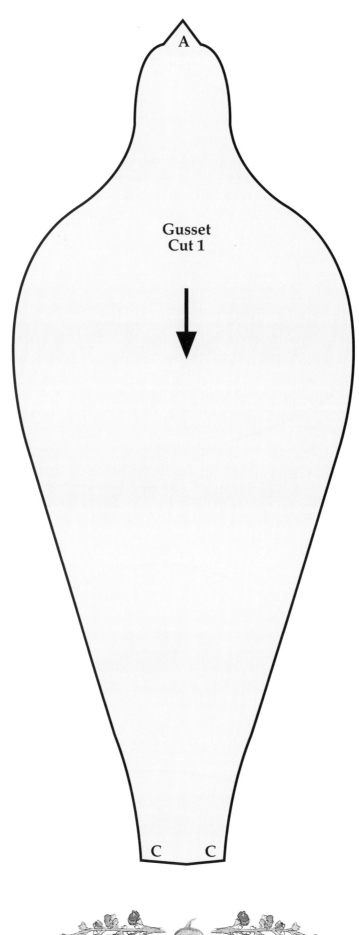

A

Gusset
Cut 1

C   C

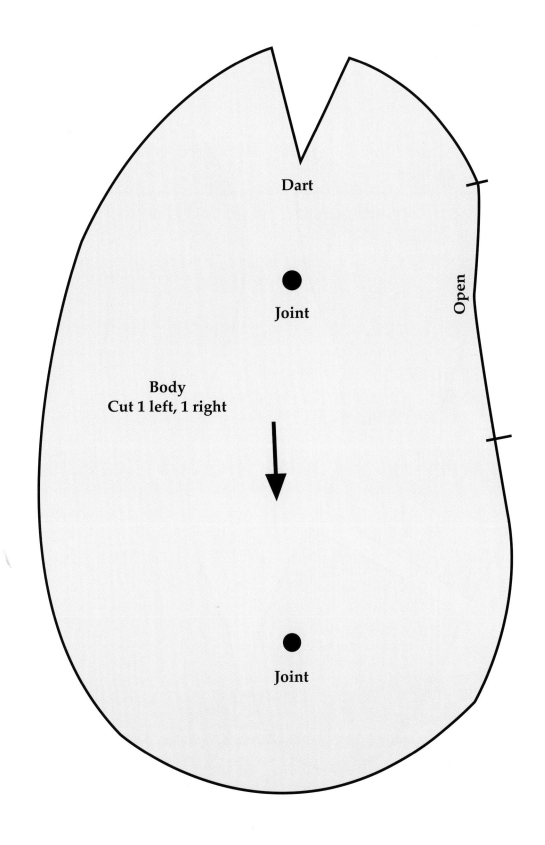

Dart

Joint

Open

Body
Cut 1 left, 1 right

Joint

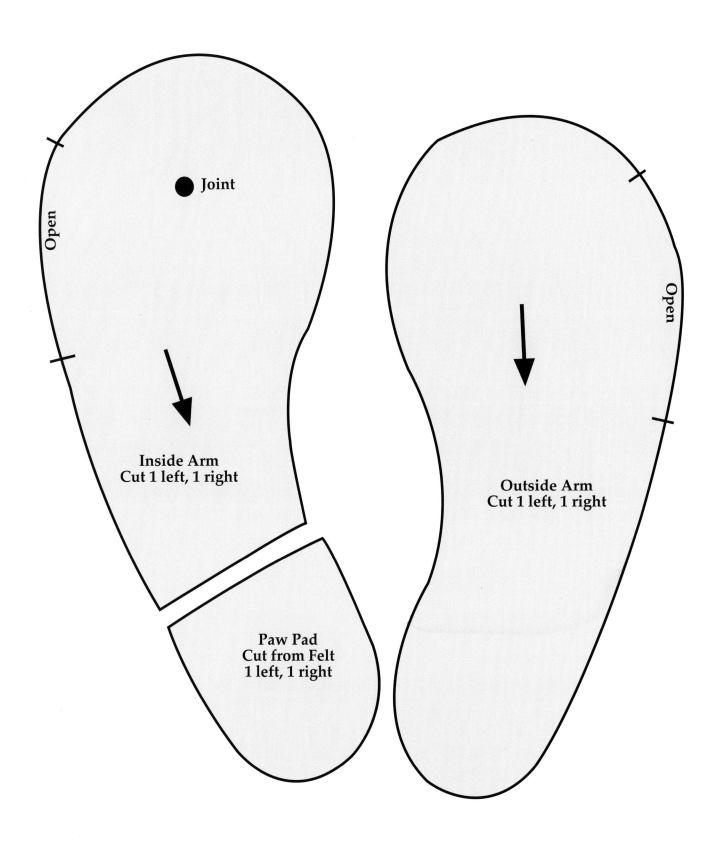

Joint

Open

Inside Arm
Cut 1 left, 1 right

Paw Pad
Cut from Felt
1 left, 1 right

Outside Arm
Cut 1 left, 1 right

Open

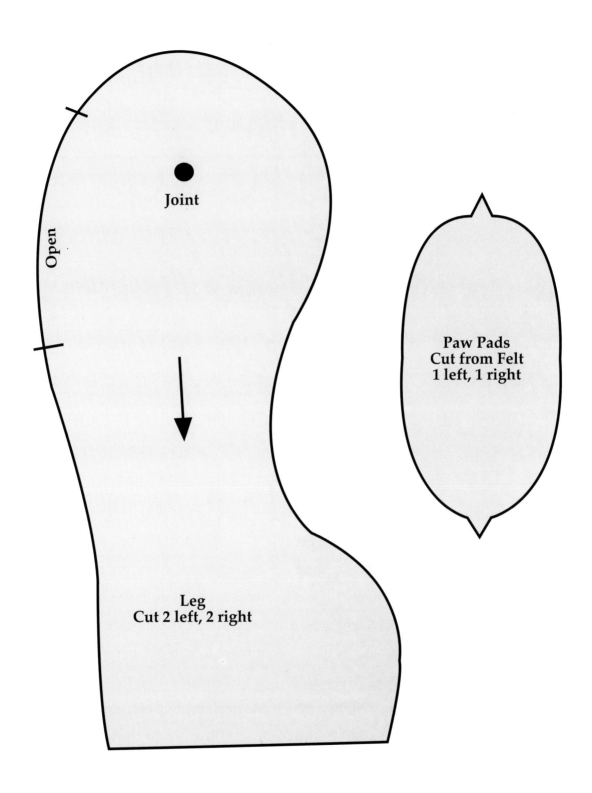

Joint

Open

Leg
Cut 2 left, 2 right

Paw Pads
Cut from Felt
1 left, 1 right

Teddy Bear Gallery

The Bearlace Cottage has been home to hundreds of Teddy Bears over the years, but most have been adopted into other homes.

Fortunately, the adoptive parents of the Teddy Bears which follow were quite understanding when word came to them about a "reunion" of sorts. With the permission of their parents, bears from just about everywhere you can name hopped aboard airplanes and trains to come back to their old stomping grounds.

Upon arrival, the bears were united with several friends who still live at Bearlace Cottage, including a few antique bears adopted by Anita Louise. Most of the bears seemed quite at home, despite their long absence, and despite the fact that they were being followed around with a camera everywhere they went.

None of the bears featured in the Teddy Bear Gallery are made from patterns found within this book. Nevertheless, seeing these bears in action could prove quite useful in refining your bear-making skills. Use this section as a guide for posing, clothing, and character ideas.

Enjoy your tour of their birthplace, and see if you don't find yourself coming up with ideas of your own!

A Teddy Bear welcome to Bearlace Cottage

Miss Ellyn chooses the proper setting for the afternoon tea

Adelaide and Norman show that the parlor is for more than entertaining guests

Miss Daphney and Auntie Amelia taking a rest before the tea party

Peaches, Daphney, Murilla and assorted antique animals prepare a Christmas meal

Peaches rolls out the dough

Eleanor irons the special tea cloth

"Once upon a time ..." says Adelaide to a beautiful antique doll-friend

An Olde bear sits by the window, waiting for the sun to set

Two Olde bears recount old times past while sitting on a table

Antique bears pose together on a mantle

An antique Ideal bear waits for tea

Sweet Buckaroo and his birdie

Grandma "Maw Maw" tries to hold Buttercup still

Rosie sits in a twig chair, looking quite elegant

Phillepe poses proudly with a beautiful antique doll

Phillepe and Miss Ellyn pose for a portrait

The End

Index

Metric Equivalency Chart

MM-Millimetres   CM-Centimetres

INCHES TO MILLIMETRES AND CENTIMETRES

INCHES	MM	CM	INCHES	CM	INCHES	CM
⅛	3	0.3	9	22.9	30	76.2
¼	6	0.6	10	25.4	31	78.7
½	13	1.3	12	30.5	33	83.8
⅝	16	1.6	13	33.0	34	86.4
¾	19	1.9	14	35.6	35	88.9
⅞	22	2.2	15	38.1	36	91.4
1	25	2.5	16	40.6	37	94.0
1¼	32	3.2	17	43.2	38	96.5
1½	38	3.8	18	45.7	39	99.1
1¾	44	4.4	19	48.3	40	101.6
2	51	5.1	20	50.8	41	104.1
2½	64	6.4	21	53.3	42	106.7
3	76	7.6	22	55.9	43	109.2
3½	89	8.9	23	58.4	44	111.8
4	102	10.2	24	61.0	45	114.3
4½	114	11.4	25	63.5	46	116.8
5	127	12.7	26	66.0	47	119.4
6	152	15.2	27	68.6	48	121.9
7	178	17.8	28	71.1	49	124.5
8	203	20.3	29	73.7	50	127.0

YARDS TO METRES

YARDS	METRES	YARDS	METRES	YARDS	METRES	YARDS	METRES	YARDS	METRES
⅛	0.11	2⅛	1.94	4⅛	3.77	6⅛	5.60	8⅛	7.43
¼	0.23	2¼	2.06	4¼	3.89	6¼	5.72	8¼	7.54
⅜	0.34	2⅜	2.17	4⅜	4.00	6⅜	5.83	8⅜	7.66
½	0.46	2½	2.29	4½	4.11	6½	5.94	8½	7.77
⅝	0.57	2⅝	2.40	4⅝	4.23	6⅝	6.06	8⅝	7.89
¾	0.69	2¾	2.51	4¾	4.34	6¾	6.17	8¾	8.00
⅞	0.80	2⅞	2.63	4⅞	4.46	6⅞	6.29	8⅞	8.12
1	0.91	3	2.74	5	4.57	7	6.40	9	8.23
1⅛	1.03	3⅛	2.86	5⅛	4.69	7⅛	6.52	9⅛	8.34
1¼	1.14	3¼	2.97	5¼	4.80	7¼	6.63	9¼	8.46
1⅜	1.26	3⅜	3.09	5⅜	4.91	7⅜	6.74	9⅜	8.57
1½	1.37	3½	3.20	5½	5.03	7½	6.86	9½	8.69
1⅝	1.49	3⅝	3.31	5⅝	5.14	7⅝	6.97	9⅝	8.80
1¾	1.60	3¾	3.43	5¾	5.26	7¾	7.09	9¾	8.92
1⅞	1.71	3⅞	3.54	5⅞	5.37	7⅞	7.20	9⅞	9.03
2	1.83	4	3.66	6	5.49	8	7.32	10	9.14